Demas Barnes

From the Atlantic to the Pacific

Demas Barnes

From the Atlantic to the Pacific

ISBN/EAN: 9783741180859

Manufactured in Europe, USA, Canada, Australia, Japa

Cover: Foto ©Andreas Hilbeck / pixelio.de

Manufactured and distributed by brebook publishing software (www.brebook.com)

Demas Barnes

From the Atlantic to the Pacific

FROM THE

ATLANTIC TO THE PACIFIC,

OVERLAND.

A SERIES OF LETTERS,

BY

DEMAS BARNES,

DESCRIBING A TRIP FROM

NEW YORK, VIA CHICAGO, ATCHISON, THE GREAT PLAINS, DENVER, THE ROCKY MOUNTAINS, CENTRAL CITY, COLORADO, DAKOTA, PIKE'S PEAK, LARAMIE PARK, BRIDGER'S PASS, SALT LAKE CITY, UTAH, NEVADA, AUSTIN, WASHOE, VIRGINIA CITY, THE SIERRAS AND CALIFORNIA, TO SAN FRANCISCO,

THENCE HOME,

BY ACAPULCO, AND THE ISTHMUS OF PANAMA.

NEW YORK:
D. VAN NOSTRAND, No. 192 BROADWAY.
1866.

MY DEAR MOTHER:

If blessings brighten as they take their flight, friends become precious in proportion as distance between them increases. Amid the varied duties of my life which have called me from the associations of childhood—as I have wandered in the wilderness—have stood upon the solitary mountain's peak—been surrounded by dangers, or have battled the storm upon the far-distant ocean, my thoughts have always fondly turned to you. Please to receive this token of remembrance, and feel that when these letters were penned, although you were distant in person, you were near me in thought.

YOUR SON.

INTRODUCTORY REMARKS.

From 1862 to '5, the mineral interests of the Western Territories were attracting the general attention of business men throughout the world. Well-authenticated representations of the fabulous production of Gold and Silver in Colorado and Nevada, were passing from mouth to mouth, and reiterated through the press in such a manner as to turn incredulity into belief, and to secure investments from the most cautious. I have never had faith in *distant* enterprises of any kind—not from want of intrinsic merit, but from general disbelief in the competency of management. Gradually, however, I became interested in Gold Mines in Colorado, Silver in Nevada, and Quicksilver in California. My associates had made me President of several companies, and I felt it to be my duty to the public and to myself, to *know, first-handed,* just what could be truthfully said in favor of these properties. At great sacrifice to my local interests, and with great expectations, I started to traverse the Continent on a tour of inspection. Had my opinions been confirmed, it would have made more than a million dollars difference to me. I have to add, that since my return I have not disposed of, or offered to dispose of, one foot or share of my mineral property, except in connection with these full statements.

While pursuing the above object, I communicated the following hurried letters to my friends, through the *Brooklyn Eagle*. Numerous applications have been made for copies, which I could not furnish; and, at this late day, I have consented to reprint them in this form.

I claim for these letters one only merit—fidelity. They are a true, plain statement of the country as it is. We have been so long educated to believe that "Westward the star of Empire takes its way," that we fail to realize that the resources of the country may not increase as we proceed towards the setting sun. Few travellers have cared to correct this opinion. If I stand alone to-day, I shall not when the subject is better understood; and these letters may be the means of saving others from sad disappointment.

DEMAS BARNES.

BROOKLYN, *December* 12, 1866.

From the Atlantic to the Pacific.

OVERLAND.

I.

COMFORTS OF STAGING—CROPS—TEMPERATURE.

DENVER, COLORADO TERRITORY, *June* 21, 1865.

I HAD not deemed it a great undertaking for *another* to cross the Continent overland, but when I sit here midway, at the foot of the Rocky Mountains, the habits of my life changed—all connection with the accumulated interests of many years of toil suspended, social ties sundered, kind friends and loved ones far behind me, with rugged hills, parched deserts, and lonely wastes far, far ahead, I do feel it is a great undertaking for *me*—for any one. Many friends said they envied me my trip, would themselves like to go, etc. I do not doubt their sincerity—I have thought so myself—but I beg to undeceive them. It is not a *pleasant*, but it is an *interesting* trip. The conditions of one man's running stages to make money, while another seeks to ride in them for pleasure, are not in harmony to produce comfort. Coaches will be overloaded, it will rain, the dust will drive, baggage will be left to the storm, passengers will get sick, a gentleman of gallantry will hold the baby, children will cry, nature demands sleep, passengers will get angry, the drivers will swear, the sensitive will shrink, rations will give out, potatoes become worth a gold dollar each, and not to be had at that, the water brackish, the whiskey abominable, and the dirt almost unendurable. I have just finished six days and nights of this thing; and I am free to say, until I forget a great many things now very visible to me, I shall not undertake it again. Stop over nights? No you wouldn't. To sleep on the sand floor of a one-story sod or adobe hut, without a chance to wash, with miserable food, uncongenial companionship, loss of seat in a coach until one comes empty, etc., won't work. A through-ticket and fifteen inches of seat, with a fat man on one side, a poor widow on the other, a baby in your lap, a bandbox over your head, and three or four more persons immediately in front, leaning against your knees, makes the picture, as well as your sleeping place, for the trip—but of all this when I come to it.

This letter should have been written from Atchison, but I had not the time. Those who constantly travel are familiar with our country east of the

Mississippi river; but many do not travel, and are now receiving their first impressions. I shall not weary you with detail, but take the trip as I find it, from New York to San Francisco, June 7th, 1865. The New York railroads are not as crowded as they were last season. Too much rain has fallen for corn east of Syracuse. Many fields must be replanted, with chance not to ripen, or the crop is a failure. Other cereals look finely, and little change to Central Michigan. In the vicinity of Rochester, and throughout our richest agricultural districts, many women may be seen tilling the soil as regular field-hands. I could but remark the contrast between this and when I was a boy, of the same section. All were then more on a level, and a woman's position was respected. Now, the accumulation of money by the few—an investment in untaxable 7-30's—removes the happy patriot and owner thereof from common sympathy with the masses; while the widow's boy, killed in battle, and the high taxes upon calico, brooms, and bonnets, which she is bound to pay, makes her a peasant and a hireling—one of the beauties of war and a national debt. Oh! dear, deluded people! did you ever think of European *caste*, what it means, how it is created, and who it affects? A few years will teach some new political lessons in this country.

The oil fever is not yet dead. New derricks are

going up, and wells are going down, through Western New York, Ohio, Canada, Michigan, Illinois, etc. I do not learn of any considerable success.

Crops are much more forward from Adrian, Michigan, west to Galesburg, Illinois, from which place south to Quincy, and west to St. Joseph, they are about the same as in Western New York —say a difference of two weeks. The atmospheric influences affecting the isothermal line in a perfectly level country, are very interesting and astonishing to a person seeking a home, or caring to know the cause of a very singular effect. Washington is in the same latitude with San Francisco; New York with Naples; Quebec with Paris; while populous London is opposite frozen Labrador, and St. Petersburg corresponds with the lower part of Greenland!

My dear lady friends, when we passed those numerous little lakes in Southern Michigan, filled with beautiful pond lilies, how I thought of your rosy cheeks, pouting lips, and terrific waterfalls! I wish every lady in the house where I live, had to have one of these exquisite lilies in her hair at every evening's dinner. What a glorious punishment for being pretty!

II.

CHICAGO—SANITARY FAIR—GENERAL OBSERVATIONS—ST. JOSEPH.

DENVER, COLORADO TERRITORY, *June* 21, 1865.

NEXT to New York, Chicago may be considered the typical American city. More changes have taken place there in my two years' absence than have been produced in Hartford, Albany, etc., in twenty. Its buildings are metropolitan—its hotels are numerous and first class—its business immense —its theatres splendid—its women beautiful—its water pure—ice clear—streets straight—and everything appears to be on the luxurious, loud order. Chicago has the best pavements in the United States, known as Nicholson pavements. Eight years ago I saw them being laid. Pieces of two-inch plank twelve inches long are saturated with composition, placed endwise upon a concrete foundation set one and a half inches apart, the seams filled with macadamizing material. They are smooth, ornamental, clean, and, what they are intended for, noiseless and easy for horses. They have stood the test and are durable. Do not suppose, dear Mr. Alderman, that Chicago cannot test a pavement as well as Broadway. Policemen are kept at the corners of Lake street to hurry on the crowd. Our Broadway pavement ought to be indicted as a nuisance for cruelty to animals. What a discomfort—what an outrage—what a cruelty it is! Every paper in the Metropolitan District should keep a stereotype article at the head of a column denouncing it, until it is changed.

Of course I attended the great Sanitary Fair—was induced to go sight-seeing after lions. Well, we saw them—lions, elephants, Rebecca at the well, a place for a fountain without water, the stars and stripes, some perfumery, corn starch, churns, bed quilts, plantation bitters, baby jumpers, daguerreotypes, the Lord's prayer written by a soldier with his toes, and many other equally rare, select, and wonderful works of art and nature. Among them, imported for the occasion, and as kind of trump cards, were sandwiched in, Generals Grant, Sherman, and Hooker. As I had been solicited to contribute to this fair, and had done so with most charitable intent, I improved the occasion to look the institution over, and I take this occasion to say, I think it quite time that these expensive begging abortions were played out, discountenanced, discouraged, and denounced. Let people disburse their charities their own way; but as to begging of other people, and themselves receiving the credit, after deducting enormous expenses, it is not creditable, moral, or just.

We took cars westward at twelve midnight; were made quite comfortable by a colored boy in a sleeping-car. In the morning, requesting to be called early to see the country, I passed him a half dollar, and found the commercial value of Eastern men to be very great. "You lives Down-East, I reckon, masser—Bosting or New York?" "Yes," I replied, "I reside in New York, and why did you think so?" "Cause, masser, yese Eastern gemmen is sort a careless with yer money. The feller in the other car thought he was goin' to get yer; but I kept good watch, yer know, and told yer how nice my car was—yah!" "Yes, I remember. Where are *you* from?" I continued. "Ise pretty considerably from the State of Missouri. If yer wants anything at the depot, masser, just call on me." I hope my Eastern friends will sustain the reputation they appear to have acquired with these poor unfortunate fellows, who gaze their eyes out of their sockets for a few dimes.

Orchards, trees, hedges, houses, etc., are vastly increasing in Illinois. The farms are upon such a magnificent scale as to create a home-feeling, and one of national pride. The Central Park contains eight hundred and sixty acres. We passed corn fields, many of them more than half as large as the Park, with rows as straight as an arrow, and so long they blend together in the distance.

With so scant a water power, and an open

prairie furnishing wind, I am much surprised that windmills are not used upon every farm. They are cheap, well adapted for threshing, pumping, churning, sawing wood, grinding, etc. Were I without business, I think I could make an easy and rapid fortune introducing them.

Crossing the Mississippi river at Quincy, you are pretty lucky to escape casualty, and reach Palmyra Junction, on the Hannibal and St. Joseph Railroad—eleven miles, in three hours. The road is in terrible condition, runs slowly, and gives one the worth of his money in perpendicular jolts. The country is mostly prairie, poorly cultivated, but rich soil, and generally well drained. You do not see a good Eastern farm-house through the State. Land can be bought very low—say eight to twenty dollars per acre; just as good as will command double that in Illinois. Government block-houses stand near each bridge. Much damage has been done by the hostile forces along this route. Many fugitives, women and children, are returning to their distant homes. Our people bear these misfortunes with much better fortitude than we could suppose.

St. Joseph is not up to the standard of most Western cities, although of great importance and large business—greatly scattered. It claims 15.000 inhabitants. Elwood, on the western bank, was at one time pushed by its energetic founder, A. R.

Elwood, Esq., of Otsego county, New York, as an imposing rival; but it is on low ground, and the public are not yet able to appreciate its supposed advantages.

A railroad, some twenty-six miles south, takes us opposite Atchison. We waited in the omnibus one full hour for the ferry-boat to start across for us. Time is of very little account here. The people seem to be impressed with the idea that the world was not made in a minute, and that another day will come. This brings us to Atchison, the starting point of the overland stage. It is certainly the last place a man would ever live in for pleasure. The ground is terribly washed and gullied out, the surface uneven, earth sticky, and the whole appearance desolate and uninviting. Atchison claims four thousand inhabitants; I do not give it two thousand. My friend Butterfield will excuse the truth in this matter. My next starts me over the plains, and where the interest of the trip commences.

III.

DENVER—THE PLAINS—GENERAL APPEARANCE—STORMS—
A LITTLE ABOUT GOLD—ATMOSPHERIC PHENOMENA—
WATER-SPOUTS—ANCHORING THE STAGE.

DENVER, *June* 25, 1865.

THE Indians have interfered with the running of the stages west of this, and it is uncertain when I shall be able to proceed. I have visited the mines in the mountains at Central City and Black Hawk, and returned here to wait my chances.

I am an average reader, but have never seen the Western plains and the incidents of this route correctly described. Colton and Mitchell both locate Denver in the mountains, while it is on the plains, twelve miles from the slightest show of a hill. What it was ever located here for is more than I can decipher. The circulars and time-tables of the stage company have but little regard to exact distances, route, etc., while verbal information, acquired from residents and ordinary messengers, is wholly unreliable. In fact, a person learns to appreciate Talleyrand's definition of language, "that it is made to conceal, not to utter, the truth," by a short sojourn among such a romantic and heterogeneous population as here exists. They literally deal in "great expectations," and discount the results at the first opportunity. Just think of it—one dollar a quire for the paper I write upon, ten cents apiece for eggs—at wholesale—ninety dollars for transporting sixty pounds of baggage! Of course they are in a hurry to point you to a "blossom rock"—gold certain—a hole in the hill twelve feet deep, and consider they give you a bargain at fifty thousand dollars. Ten thousand carcasses of poor overworked animals, marking the highway over seven hundred miles of parching, treeless plain, is a small matter—while gold is before them, around them, everywhere. It is almost impossible not to partake of the general enthusiasm, for you hear gold discussed morning, noon, all night, and far into the next day. It is no myth. You see it—you select specimens for your cabinet—you hear the turning of the water-wheels, the puffing of the engines, the pounding of the stamps, the clatter of the pans—you see the steam of the retort and assay—you hold the pure golden nuggets in your hands, your eyes dilate, your mouth waters, and you think—what gold has done for the world, what we would have done without gold, what man will not do for gold, and how happy you would be, and how proud and happy would be those dear ones far away dependent upon you for existence, were you its possessor. Dear reader, it is hard to break the charm, or wake the dreamer—so, with generous feeling, I leave the gold mines of Colorado until I approach them in proper order, promising them a candid description, and now return to my last stopping-place.

I shall not be prolix, but too much brevity will fail to convey a practical view of the immensity of our subject. The water poured into the ocean by the Mississippi river averages nineteen and a half trillions (19,500,000,000,000) cubic feet per year, while three times this amount is evaporated in the atmosphere and absorbed in the soil. All of this multiplied vast amount reaches the earth in rain or snow, condensed by the snow peaks of the Rocky Mountains as it passes eastward from the Pacific Ocean. Holding this fact in view, and returning for a moment to Lake Michigan and Indiana, the line of prairie country, and you will realize the atmospheric and physical influences which mark the characteristics of these immense plains. The eastern portion of the great prairie system of the United States presents almost a dead level surface, interspersed with forests, preventing devastating winds and the wash of vegetable decay which enriches the land. Wood gradually disappears, the land rises and becomes more rolling, and the streams swift, as you proceed west, until soon after crossing the Missouri river small timber is only seen skirting the water courses. From Julesburg, three hundred miles to the gorges of the mountains, such a thing as a tree, shrub, or bush is not to be seen. The result is, the land is swept by the most terrific gales, and the soil, being free and light, is either driven in clouds of dust and sand, or washed by bursting clouds of rain into the ravines and rivers, thence to the Balize and Gulf of Mexico—thus denuding these plains of vegetable life, and creating the rich alluvial bottom lands of the Mississippi. It is geologically proven that the land, from the junction of the Ohio and Mississippi rivers down to the Gulf, has been formed in this way from what was once the Gulf of Mexico. Evidence is here indisputably furnished in what are denominated the "Buttes"—when the soil is of a more solid character, composed of gravel or clay, small plateaus or peaks rise silent and alone in the prairies—with sides washed like the banks of gulches. Bear in mind, then, that this is not the land flowing with milk and honey—that we have embarked in a semi-barren plain—with a climate more fickle than I had believed existed on the face of the earth. It was near evening of our second day, calm, delightful, but hot. I was sitting with the driver outside, holding an umbrella to protect me from the tropical heat while in but a linen coat. A cloud appeared in the south-east, a sudden and intensely cold breeze struck us, and I will venture to say the thermometer sank thirty degrees in ten minutes; the whole heavens were streaked with forked lightnings; the wind rose to a hurricane that seemed about to snap and start the very sods from the earth, while as to rain—it might have rained harder before, and it might have rained harder since, but I didn't happen to be out in it. A ship might as well proceed under full sail in a typhoon, as a stage across the plains in one of these storms. The teamsters understand themselves, wheel the horses' heads from the wind, and lay to until their fury is passed. This is no fancy sketch. Twice during our passage were we compelled to make this kind of an uncertain anchorage. Stages are frequently capsized. When occurring in the night time, as did one of ours, and which is more usually the case—the Egyptian darkness, interspersed with vivid lightning the most incessant I ever witnessed — reverberating thunder that seemed to make the very earth quake and tremble —with no voice audible above the clatter of the pelting rain—one is strongly reminded that home would be a very comfortable place to be in.

Immense fresh gullies and washes are thus constantly occurring. A high wind is of nightly occurrence at this season of the year. It rains once or twice almost every day; it is disagreeably cold once in two days, and intensely warm in about the same proportion. The scene shifts with the rapidity of a drama, and a panorama of beauty presents itself, to which neither the pen of Irving nor the pencil of Hogarth could do justice. Onward bound!

IV.

THE START — FARE — HOME REFLECTIONS — PILGRIMS — GAME — FORDING STREAMS — SIGHT OF THE ROCKY MOUNTAINS.

DENVER, COL., *June* 26, 1865.

I HAVE run a little ahead of my diary. Ten miles out of Atchison, you are fairly in the prairie wilds, and make no town of account until you reach Denver, six hundred and forty miles. For convenience of forage the overland transportation and emigration trains take all the western water courses and start from Leavenworth, Nebraska City, Atchison, St. Joseph, Omaha, &c., so that no *one* route gives a full comprehension of this business. Butterfield's overland despatch will send out thirty thousand yoke (60,000 head!) of cattle this season, averaging six yoke to the wagon. They reach Denver, in say forty days.

The fare from Atchison to Salt Lake is $350. Baggage over twenty-five pounds, $1 50 per pound —meals extra. I found them to commence at $1 and advance to $2. All this is entirely different from the information given me at the Stage office in New York.

It was eight o'clock in the morning. A whip

cracked—a heavy Concord stage wheeled in front of the office; on it was painted "Overland." Childish though it might have been, I felt sad; it was a long distance. I was running from letters, from home, from friends. Life is not so full of pleasure that we can afford to put three thousand miles between us and our dearest heart treasures and not feel irresolute and pained. Our effects were soon loaded, 1,600 pounds of Mail in the Coot, our baggage on top exposed to the storm. Hear me, Mr. Halliday; all the protection it had was extemporized by the passengers in the shape of coats and shawls —not even a cheap tarpaulin or an old blanket. I was just taking my seat when a messenger handed me a telegraphic dispatch from New York. I think I should have secretly rejoiced had it announced some slight casualty demanding my return. No, it was merely—"all's well." I breathed back a silent *memoria in eterna*, and we were on our way, ascending, descending, for six and a half days over the most beautiful landscape my eyes ever rested upon. The rugged, hard, sublime mountain scenery has its charms, but to me the softened, genial, finished, smooth outlines of a cooling sea of land, sinking in the horizon, and colored by the different hues of the atmosphere, awakens sentiments of a different and far more agreeable character. Space as well as immensity, utility as well as sublimity, life in place of barrenness, affection instead of frigidity, are the sentiments in accordance with our emotional natures, calling us nearer to humanity, and striking cords of far sweeter strains.

The few scattered farms of the first day out present little of interest. Houses of logs—a little wheat and hemp, small and poorly cultivated; potatoes none. The great feature of the Plains is the transportation trains, usually consisting of thirty to fifty wagons, five yoke each. The wagons have high boxes, covered with white canvass drawn over high wooden bows. As they wind their slow course over the serpentine roads and undulating surface in the distance, a mile in extent (I saw one train five miles long), the effect is poetic, grand, beautiful. They select a high position for camping, draw the wagons in a circle, enclosing say a quarter, half, or full acre, the exterior serving as a fort, the inside as a camp, and a place wherein to drive the animals in case of danger, and to yoke or harness them for the next trip. One of these camps, seen at sundown, with night-fires kindled, and from five hundred to a thousand head of animals feeding near by, is well worth a long visit to behold. Of course the herd is watched by outriding muleteers. The trains start at four o'clock in the morning, camp at ten, and proceed again from two until six. Emigrants, or pilgrims as they are here termed, have lighter loads, and have only from two to four yoke—one yoke generally being of milch cows, answering a double and useful purpose. It is wonderful to see the number of farmers with their families and household goods thus migrating to further western homes. Those we saw were principally from the States of Illinois, Indiana, and Missouri, and were either bound for Utah, Oregon, or Washington Territory. We estimated from four to five hundred wagons passed each day—one day at least a thousand. This is only *one* route.

The roads were heavy and we made but eighty miles the first twenty-four hours; the route, bearing north by west, crosses into Nebraska at Cottonwood creek, one hundred and seven miles out, and reaches Fort Kearney on the Platte river, two hundred and sixty miles. Prairie fowl, quail, snipe, etc., are seen in abundance, though singular to say we get no taste of any at the stations. At the crossing of the Big Blue creek the driver put our feet about one foot under water without notice, and thought it a good joke. The dust and mud already in the coach, added to the crackers, etc., composing our luncheons, the small bags and bundles necessarily so deposited, made anything but an agreeable mess the balance of the way. This, like most other rivers this way, is a swift, unreliable stream, with steep banks. It rises sometimes two to six feet in an hour and becomes thirty feet deep. In two days it is nearly dry.

From Kearney the houses are principally of sod or adobe, one story high, and generally without floors—stations from ten to fifteen miles apart, horses good, four to a coach, eating stations about two per day, meals as good as could be expected, excepting total absence of potatoes.

From about one hundred and fifty miles out, our dignity was much enhanced by a government cavalry escort of two or four horsemen with each stage night and day. The Indians have committed terrible depredations along three hundred miles of the route, burned and pillaged everything, destroyed six thousand bushels of corn at Julesburg, burned hundreds of thousands of dollars' worth of wagons, merchandise, &c. One or two ranches, as they call farms here, had erected thick sod breastworks, perforated for rifle shot, and stood the siege. Stock was either all lost or had to be protected in corrals in same manner.

The two regiments stationed on this line are Confederate volunteers from Louisiana and Tennessee. It is the universal testimony at every station that before they came here, the soldiers plundered and stole more than the Indians. Since they have been here no single theft has occurred. They are very courteous, and prefer remaining in service until things get more quiet at home. We did not encounter any Indians, but saw many remains of their barbarity.

I could not ascertain that any buffaloes have been captured here for two or three years. At least I saw none, though their old hard-beaten paths and wallowing holes were numerous. Of wolves we saw none, antelope we did see a few, and wanted much to eat them, the beef being horrid and tough. The Platte river is very straight, from a quarter to one mile wide from the Missouri to Denver. It is shoal most of the season and has no capacity for navigation. Its current is rapid. The soil becomes more barren and wasted as we approach the mountains, being a portion of the way almost a desert. As wood or bushes disappear, a beautiful, hardy, but prickly and unnutritious cactus in all variety of colors comes upon the scene and grows clear into the mountain gorges. I had never seen it cultivated in our Eastern gardens. It is equal to any tropical specimens of our conservatories, and stands a climate twenty to thirty degrees below zero. If not found on my return, I have arranged to have some sent me. It is the only thing worthy to be called a flower on the prairies. Other floral specimens few and coarse. I have heard travellers extol the floral beauties of the prairies. I do not find them.

A large portion of the prairies are good for nothing, and never can be cultivated. They are cold and bare in winter—dry and washed in summer. The great enemy of the soil is the clouds which gather in the mountains and burst—not rain—carrying everything before them. A channel one thousand feet wide was two years ago forced through the city of Denver, and now lies a plateau of sand, crossed by bridges—the town divided. The great want of prairies is wood and water. The bottom lands may be irrigated—the higher lands cannot be, except by artesian wells, the expense of which will not be warranted for many generations. Thirty feet wells, however, usually find water for drinking purposes, which could be raised by windmills, if desirable, but insufficient for irrigating land. Never look for dense population under these circumstances. It raises a question respecting our future political relations with the Pacific States, which each may discuss for himself.

I undertake to say that a railroad is a political necessity, whether it pays financially or not. I have before remarked that for three hundred miles east of the Rocky Mountains no tree or shrub, and but little grass, appears. For a portion of the distance there is literally no grass. I doubt if trees could be made to withstand the terrific winds even if they had soil to grow in. Even hay and all vegetables have to be transported from the east. The emigrants have to carry their wood and gather buffalo chips to cook their meals with. Insensibly we have made an elevation to Denver of over four thousand feet. Seasons must be short and farming inducements small.

At daybreak of our fifth day, we were at Brandy Station on the Platte river, and distinctly saw in the distance, the white-capped summits of the Rocky Mountains—those far off mythical hills of our childhood. They looked, say thirty miles distant. We travelled all that day until three o'clock next morning, and were still sixty-five miles to the nearest point first visible. We had seen these ranges over one hundred and seventy-five miles in an air-line! They sparkle in the sunlight, rising from the plain, like gems upon a lady's bosom. The rarification of the atmosphere extends the vision to double its capacity upon water. My next will carry me into the mountains, down a shaft, out of a tunnel, with a piece of gold ore in my hands, and if not a brick in my hat, at least an idea in my head.

V.

Denver—Golden City—Black Hawk—Central City—Gold Mining—Nary Nugget—High Up in the World.

Denver, Col., *June* 27, 1865.

Denver is a square, proud, prompt little place, which, like Pompey's Pillar, is surrounded by immensity. It is better built than St. Joseph or Atchison, has fine brick stores, four churches, a good seminary, two theatres, two banks, plenty of gambling shops, a fine United States mint, which I observed had nothing to do, and which, as near as I could ascertain, had actually coined the vast amount of forty thousand dollars in a whole year! and the most abominable hotels a person ever put his feet into. There being no wood, brick becomes a necessity for building purposes—hence the character of its buildings. Population claimed, six thousand. I am sorry to cut them down to four thousand, but that is more than they can count, unless they add the flies, of which at least several millions dine with us every day. I have omitted to speak of one feature in our travels which curdles the blood at every step. The cruelty to animals by the brutal drivers is perfectly awful. Each teamster carries a raw-hide lash about nine feet long, one and a half inches in diameter at the belly, attached to a short stock or handle, folded over his shoulder, which he uses upon the poor, willing, overworked dumb beasts with apparent delight, and frequently draws blood at every stroke. The concussion is like the snap of a pistol. I wish the drivers—the most blasphemous wretches that ever disgraced a language—might have one good blow to see how they would like it. The seven hundred miles I have travelled have been literally lined with the bones and carcasses of domestic animals.

We again cross the plains about fourteen miles to the foot hills of the mountains, where Clear Creek forces its way through, and where Denver should have been located. Irrigating canals are here in operation, some five, others fifteen miles long, and at points. I am informed, some crops are grown. I saw none.

The grasshoppers had not left a spire of anything green standing. It was the same last year. Some attempts are now (June 26th) being made to replant corn, potatoes, &c.—a sorry prospect.

About two miles up in the mountains on the course of Clear Creek, is a little plateau where stands Golden City—the capital of the territory. It probably contains seventy buildings, all of cheap character. What the inhabitants do to support themselves, beyond those engaged in teaming, I could not ascertain.

The gulch, ravine, or cañon, as it may be called, is rough and uninviting. The mountains, at first, show but few indications of forest, but as you advance, a few straggling pines appear, which increase for say fifty miles, but interspersed with bald-top hills. Everything is side-hill and edgewise one way or the other, and the labor of securing wood is immense. I heard of a species of goat which always has its right legs shorter than those upon the other side for the purpose of grazing upon the side-hill. His face must always be one way and he gradually winds round and up the mountain. In his efforts to turn round, he tips over, and lands in the gulf below. This is probably the reason why the species do not increase in number. I can only say I did not, myself, dine from any such goat steak.

Coal of indifferent quality has been discovered at the foot of the mountains; this will no doubt improve.

We arrive at Black Hawk and Central City, which are and should be one, after eight hours of heavy staging from Denver. I could not decline the generous hospitality of my friends, Messrs. Lee, Judd and Kinney, and made myself immediately at home. An area of, say, six miles in diameter, contains a population of some ten to fifteen thousand souls, mostly crowded into narrow gulches, branching off in different directions at

Black Hawk. This vicinity is said to be rich in gold, lead, copper, sulphur, iron, antimony, cobalt, arsenic, &c. Gold alone is being worked; there is no myth, exaggeration, or deceit; they have it here, they say, in inexhaustible quantities.

The hill-sides are dotted everywhere with tunnels and shafts; the lodes are frequently but a few feet from each other. They will run from two to six feet wide at one hundred feet deep, and will *assay* from $50 to $200 per ton. To stop just here would leave the thing very handsome. But there is another side to it; many mills are stopped, many lodes are not being worked: what is the reason? Mill-masters reply, "labor is too high." No, that is not it. Ore which fairly assays $80 per ton, will *work* but $20; that's what's the matter. They do not know how to get the gold out. I find *nine* different processes working at this place alone, each claiming to be the best; yet the result of all shows that something is wanting still. Do not be alarmed; I, too, may have gold lodes to sell! I wish to encourage scientific, practical research, so that when I sell or work them the gold can be got out. This is fast coming, but as almost all lodes require different treatment, I am content to wait a little, and let some one else do the experimenting. Some cheap desulphurizing process will no doubt come nearest to a scientific basis. Then, again, capital invested is too anxious for returns. No doubt the sensible way would be, first to secure your lodes, open your veins, test your ore at some neighbor's mill; when you have got a good thing, encountered and conquered the inevitable poor "cap work," then pile up your ore, and let the air, the best desulphurizer in the world, work upon it one year—you have saved the money invested in a mill, have improved your ore twenty per cent., have had time to watch improvements, and know what kind of machinery you require, and are now prepared to put it up without mistake, at much less than original cost—will have swindled nobody with false hopes, and will have acted like men. The values, gentlemen, are here, but don't forget Mrs. Glass's recipe for cooking a hare: "First, catch your hare." First, get your ore. Trace these applications. You will find but few exceptions in the result. The present mills may do well by running $20 to $30 per ton; saving the "tailings," and next year running them again with better results. Too much waste exists in this respect. It is slightly expensive to dig, crib, and raise ore out of a shaft. I descended three hundred and seventy-five feet, and then wandered off several hundred feet in the drift on the Gregory lode. Such enterprises are not child's play, by any means. It costs something to live here, and those who won't work must travel. Most everything comes from the States, and costs by the pound: Flour, 20 cents;

salt, 25; rice, 40; cheapest sugar, 35; coffee, 60 to 85; common molasses, $4 50 per gallon; eggs, $1 25 per dozen; ham, 50 cents; lard, 40; beans, 35; corn, 20; potatoes, 25; butter, 60; hay, 10; &c.

Many good companies are moving straight along in fine feather. The "Black Hawk" have been running fifty-five stamps for a long time, and will soon start equal to forty more. "The New York," "Ophir," "Naragansett," "Chase," "Consolidated," "Union," "United States," "Briggs," &c., are among the best, but are probably no better than others I did not learn so much about. The new "Continental," now nearly completed, will be one of the finest mills in the territory. It is to be operated by Colonel Clark's new process, and I doubt not will be a success. The peculiar forms of the sulphurets and pyrites containing the ore of this locality, makes the method of treatment really the great and only question.

We are about eleven thousand feet high; the air is very rare; I readily get out of breath, and find climbing ladders and chasing stages up hill very fatiguing. The suction-pump will lift water but about twenty-two feet; on the seaboard thirty-one to thirty-two is the standard. I see but little variation in the thermometer. They claim it is very healthy, and say they had to import the first corpse to start a burying-ground. I find here two daily and weekly papers, three banks, many good stores, and fine schools, under the influence of Mayor Kinney, who thinks schools the greatest inducement to secure permanent miners.

My stay here was altogether too short; but, being ticketed to Salt Lake or fight with the Indians, I was compelled to return to Denver and take my chances. As some one said about the Quakers, "The Lord may love the Indians, but I don't think he admires their conduct of late." They have taken a great fancy to white men's scalps and horses. These are the longest days, and, consequently, shortest nights. It is hardly dark at nine; a bright moon irradiates the night, and day dawns at three in the morning. Short naps, with my hand on my six-shooter, and the reassuring presence of a military escort, quiets my nerves, and would not add greatly to my insurance policy, in my estimation. The stages run on from here again, but only tri-weekly. The mail is piled up at different places, and I think the bottom of it here will hardly move for a month. I expect my Salt Lake letters are thus detained, and I shall not receive them. It is outrageous the way the public are swindled by the proprietors of this stage-route. I speak only what I know, and repeat a remark made by the agents: "Too much trouble to tear the pile out from the bottom." If I remember correctly, Mr. Halliday gets $800,000 per annum for carrying the United States mail *once a day*. This, of course, gives him a chance to run stages, carry passengers, and keep other people off the course. I have seen the stages pass through here loaded with passengers, and not carry a pound of mail, while perhaps two weeks' mail, or more, lay heaped up in the office! The passage from Atchison to Salt Lake is $350. Eight passengers would be $2,800 ; extra baggage, say $100 more.

I am to leave in the morning, unless further interrupted by Indians ; I expect to arrive in Salt Lake about July 6th, instead of 1st. as I should have done. I shall spend two days there—a few days at Austin, Nevada—Humboldt—Virginia City; thence to San Francisco—the Almaden Quicksilver Mines ; thence to the Geysers and the Sonora Quicksilver Mines, and take steamer August 1st for home. Those ladies who do not want an inside view of Brigham's harem must avoid my next letters, certain.

VI.

MOUNTAIN STREAMS—IRRIGATION—RESULT OF MINING—PRAIRIE DOGS—LARAMIE PARK—PRIMITIVE GEOLOGY—S. T. 1860 X—INDIANS—MEN KILLED.

FORT HALLECK, DAKOTA, *July* 1, 1865.

I HAVE written too rapidly and with many omissions. Instead of the more direct route, via the North Platte and Fort Laramie, we now follow up the south fork in a south-westerly direction, entering Colorado Territory, near Julesburg. At Cache-a-la-Poudre junction, the Platte makes a detour almost direct south, running for near one hundred and fifty miles, from twelve to twenty-five miles from the foot of the mountains. About every five to fifteen miles there proceeds from the mountains a swift, clear, beautiful stream, uniting as a tributary to the Platte, and affording the most magnificent system of irrigation and water power in the world. Aside from the influence of the water-spouts and its altitude, this section, between the mountains and the Platte, affords farming advantages I have seldom seen equalled. The prices obtainable for products in this section are enormous, and compensate in some degree for the inconveniences of living here. With corn and potatoes at twenty cents per pound, or $12 per bushel, this is apparent. Young farm hands obtain from $60 to $75 per month, and "found." Mechanics and miners get from $5 to $8 per day; female house servants from $30 to $50 per month, and female cooks, $60 per month and "found." Lay in your dry goods for a two-years' stay and come out with a transportation train; the balance is all profit.

The water in the western part of the plains is impregnated with alkali, causing thirst and parched lips. I do not see that it is otherwise injurious, although in dry weather water pools settle entirely away, leaving a solid crust of saleratus. In such cases cattle are frequently killed. In this section the mountain creeks are very fine.

Minute descriptions of practical mining will have no value for the majority of readers, hence I have sought to touch only upon subjects of general interest. Respecting the yield of mining in Colorado, no information can be obtained at the mint in Denver, or from any other authority here. Most of the product is sent east before being assayed. The probable approximation is, say by all processes, equal to 1,000 stamps or 3,000 tons of ore reduced per day, yielding, say $20 per ton; three hundred days per year is $6,000,000. I think that less than one quarter of the above mills are in operation, not from want of ore, but from lack of knowledge how to work it. If the total cost of mining is now equal to total receipts of $20 to $25 per ton from ore assaying $80 per ton, when the working can be made to run $60 per ton, the difference will be profit, and will again stimulate the development of other mines. The use of salt is a large item in amalgamating, which, at twenty cents per pound, is a great expense. Next comes quicksilver, indispensable in any process, which loses about three per cent. of each assay, and of which it is estimated 180,000 pounds are annually consumed in this section alone. Of the quicksilver product of the world over, ninety-five per cent. of the entire amount comes from only three mines. The opening of the Sonoma mines is very opportune, and is a source of congratulation to miners.

After six days detention at Denver, with promise of a clear coast, and seven in the coach, we left that city, but soon found ourselves with eleven passengers, and other mishaps to follow. We leave the Platte five to ten miles to our right, proceed northerly about twelve miles from the mountains for near eighty miles—then pass the first range of mountains, through what are known as the Black Hills. The snow ranges, seen from the plains, are about sixty to seventy miles beyond the first range, though appearing not more than fifteen to twenty miles from where we were riding. We could see objects more distinctly from our coach upon the side-hills of the mountains fifteen miles distant, than you can from the Battery to Staten Island, a distance of six miles. Long's Peak, higher than Pike's Peak, a hundred miles further south, bore about fifteen degrees to the north-west of us at eight o'clock in the morning. We were only apparently leaving it to the south at six P. M. We passed many prairie-dog towns, some of them of considerable extent, as had been the case throughout the extent of the plains. This is a beautiful little animal, an apparent cross between the squirrel and the woodchuck. In appearance they resemble, in miniature, the sea lion, at the Museum, being very symmetrical, well formed and smooth. They are graniverous, and are said to be good eating. I shall be willing to accept this as hearsay—for it is a fact that they live in the same holes with owls and rattlesnakes.

Our entire baggage went under water in fording Boulder Creek, and I am now trying to dry my shirts in the sun, while writing this on my valise, by the side of a hut, surrounded by a dozen or so of my disappointed travelling companions. Their conversation, adventures and jokes, would no doubt be more interesting to my readers than what I shall write. They at least demand an equal share of my attention, and frequent promises that I will report them all heroes " down home." I wish I could.

We entered the Rocky Mountains through hills not difficult of ascent, cut into rugged cañons, presenting some bold scenery—and after about twenty miles, bringing us out upon Laramie Plain, one of the most wonderful features in the physical structure of the world. To our right was Laramie Peak—to the south, the dim form of Meridian Bow Peak—ahead, was the unobstructed horizon of an undulating prairie. The distance between those two peaks is over three hundred miles; and the basin, here fenced in, almost level, upon the very summit of the Rocky Mountains, is as large as the State of Connecticut! There are several of these plains extending to the southward, known as the North, South and Middle Park. This Park is traversed by several fine water-courses running northward. Its hills are more rugged than those of the great plains east of the mountains, and produce but slight vegetation. The surface is mostly gravel and small stones, making it very severe upon the unshod cattle of the emigrant. It has been terrifically washed, and is no doubt many thousand feet below its original altitude. In places, many strata of earth and rock, which have been left there alone, assume fantastic and most interesting shapes. One place, of several miles in circumference, bore the appearance of a destroyed city. Here and there, scattered at romantic distances, leaned the shattered columns—projecting cornice—

open windows—the clean time-polished sides of what it was easy to imagine, were the temples, amphitheatres, and dwellings of an ancient race of men. I could only be reminded of the ruins of Thebes and Karnak, and almost looked for the hieroglyphic symbols to unfold the history of the particular ruin. So with the more rocky portion of the hills. Fissures are worn in the vertical strata, and columns of granite, supporting capitals, lintels, and pediment roof, stand as erect as if placed there but yesterday. Silent, solitary, and alone, they look like the monasteries of the Andalusian monks, built for retirement and seclusion in the mountain gorges,—or when more boldly located, like the castles of the feudal barons of the middle ages, where one sentinel would stand as guard against an approaching host. I would give a large price for photographic views of some half-dozen places I have seen, and am surprised I did not find them in Denver. The history of the creation of the present aspect of these hills has an imaginary interest of overpowering sublimity. Back, far back, thousands upon hundreds of thousands of years, in the Devonian period, when perhaps the Rocky Mountains, the Sierras, and the Apalachian chain, were the only land on the North American continent, we can well imagine the density of the atmosphere, the force of the winds, and the outpouring of waters, upon these defiant peaks. Solid pieces of granite, measuring two hundred thousand cubic feet, have been cast headlong and landed by the glaciers in the valleys miles away during our day. How much more mighty the forces of nature must have been, before the physical aspects of the earth fitted it for the abode of man!

I cannot fail to recount one instance of remarkable and ludicrous scenic effect. Everywhere I have been—from the White Mountains of New Hampshire, through the Middle States, across the plains—way up in the Rocky Mountains—and now out upon Laramie Park—wherever there is a frowning rock or projecting surface—that indomitable Drake has painted his cabalistic "S. T. 1860 X—Plantation Bitters." He must be insane if he expects to get his expenses back out here—although wherever I saw anything for sale, his Bitters formed a part of the stock. I paid $2 50 for a bottle on my way from Denver to Central City.

But these mountain fastnesses, rounded hills, dark ravines, and smouldering castles, answer just now a different purpose than that of exciting the imagination over the beauty of a landscape. They afford just the shelter, protection, and communication for the Indian, who, in the arts of barbarity and savage ferocity, is quite the same as when his ancestors committed the massacre of Wyoming. Somewhere up here they have, no doubt, four thousand to six thousand head of stock stolen from the white emigrants. We had whistled to keep up our courage, and tried not to believe in Indians for some time. But evidences accumulated very fast, and we were quite willing to keep our escort very near us. We were not allowed to travel nights any longer. We slept on the earth-floor of the station at Cooper Creek, soldiers guarding outside. We procured eight mules the next morning, and had proceeded six miles, when some horsemen came riding down upon us like lightning, crying "Indians."

Eleven rifles sprang to the windows, and my hair sprang to my head; the coach wheeled about so quick as nearly to tip us over—and if we did not make a race, I am no judge. We ran our mules five miles, until we intercepted an emigrant train, and also a company of cavalry. A council of war was held; it was decided to proceed. We were forty-four military and twenty civilians strong —your humble servant the only person seen on the route not provided with a Spencer or a Henry's rifle; but I had a revolver, and thought at close quarters I could take a hand. The Indians, in turn, retreated, but kept on our flanks, and killed one poor boy belonging to the military escort, who had followed them too far. We recovered his body. The diabolical wretches!—they had stripped him entirely of his clothing, dug out his eyes, torn off his scalp, opened both his breasts, took out his heart and entrails—a tribute to his bravery—cut off both his feet, cut his head nearly off, and otherwise disfigured him—leaving one bullet in his head and eight arrows through his body. I have one arrow, which I shall carry home. They afterwards intercepted us at the crossing of a gulch and at the brow of a hill. We were in for a fight, and drew up in line. I felt my day had come, and wished myself home. My life is of too much importance to others, if not to myself, to throw it away ignobly, fighting Indians! I much prefer to be a living coward than a dead hero. But there was no return—no escape. We approached on a slow trot; got in firing range, the bullets flew from every gun. Their leader fell, and our force being large, they skedaddled as fast as they could run. They were very shrewd, and sent out small parties, endeavoring to beguile "the whites" into some place of ambush, when hundreds of their warriors would have sprung upon and hewed us to pieces! We did not follow. For me, the realizing sense of a whole scalp and a pull at my canteen was a great relief. This is only a sample of what is daily occurring. Two of our pilgrim companions were killed the same day. The stage company is minus horses, the government without a tithe of a military force, and the people without sufficient to eat. There is not force enough here to guard the stations, let alone hunting Indians. It will require sixty days to march from the river, and I do not believe things will be safe or in shape until one year from this time. Ten thousand troops are needed in this country. Allow no one who sees this to start one inch beyond Denver until things are changed. It is impossible to guess how long it will be before we can get a wagon, horses, or escort, to send us on. Were this a *through* letter, you would not get it this summer; but I shall watch my chance to forward it to Denver, and you may receive it. Tons of mail are abandoned at the different stations. I have seen it, Mr. Halliday, and my name is at your service.

VII.

LIFE AMONG THE MORMONS—MORE INDIANS—THE DESERT—AN OX IN A PIT—RAILROAD—BEAUTIFUL SCENERY—MOUNTAIN FLOWERS—SALT LAKE CITY—MORMONS—POLYGAMY—BRIGHAM YOUNG.

GREAT SALT LAKE CITY, *July* 7, 1865.

THERE is no disguising the fact, I am not in good humor. Nine days and nights jolting and pounding over the most wretched of roads, arriving here ten days behind time, finding no letters, and telegraphic communication cut off for three weeks, slightly disconcert me, interferes with my arrangements, impel me onward, and will cut my letters short. The Indians killed three instead of one man the day of our encounter near Wagon Hound Cañon. The supposition is they have been getting ready for a heavy onslaught and cleaning out in that section, as they did for a stretch of over two hundred miles east of Denver last winter and spring. The following day the fortunate arrival of a small squad of soldiers from Laramie induced the stage to try and work east. About four hundred to five hundred Indians disputed their passage; sixty mounted cavalry and two hundred armed pilgrims dared not attack them, and all put back to the best base they could obtain—the stage to our station. We deem ourselves most fortunate in having safely run the gauntlet of these fellows. This was only eighteen miles from where we lay cooped up for two days, thirteen sleeping on the one floor of a small cabin, without horses to carry us on, or soldiers to defend us. Reports were that the Indians were moving towards us. We placed our sentinels at dusk, put out our light, and waited the morning with an anxiety I had never before experienced. Each man's gun had been overhauled, and, with extra cartridges, lay by his side. I alone had but a pistol. All realized that another morning to any of our little band was very uncertain. Things were serious. As I stealthily took from my pocket and wistfully gazed upon the pictures of my dear and loved ones that were far away, and whose faces I might never again behold, the reminiscences of the past came crowding before me awakening holy and emotional thoughts, that made sleep impossible and the hours long. My mother, my wife, and my little Cora visibly stood before me, and with outstretched arms and beseeching looks implored and begged me to return. I could hardly contain my speech. It seemed as if I must jump from this mountain solitude to the borders of civilization at a single bound. Towards the second morning a stage with two passengers, four soldiers and two drivers, came rolling in from the west— the first for several days. Never was voice of man more welcome. I breathed freer, and as day dawned our force strengthened and danger lessened; it was wonderful how soon the fears of the past were forgotten, and how rapidly the mind engaged in new plans for the future. Morally speaking, I believe men are in earnest when they resolve to change their habits of life; but their sincerity proceeds from a cause—fear, weakness, or disappointment: remove the cause and the original instincts will prevail, and former habits be reinstated.

We spent all of the next day in trying to coax, hire, or scare the driver into a trial trip. It all seemed useless; but money is very powerful, and by sundown we had succeeded in securing nine soldiers and two drivers, and started on our way westward. A very consoling idea to a driver, that he must have another man on the box with him, that in case he gets shot some one can take the lines! Singular that mountaineers consider night the safest time to avoid Indian attacks.

Right there, say twenty-five miles east of the North Platte, commences the desert in earnest. From the Platte west to Fort Bridger, two hundred miles, is one almost uninterrupted panorama of barren hills, sandy plains, ugly tortuous ravines, and blank desolation. Patches of wild sage, rejected by animals, is the only sign of vegetation that meets the eye. I looked industriously, and am willing to qualify that, except at Pine Grove, a little oasis, I did not see a half acre of good, bad, or indifferent grazing all this distance. How the poor cattle, mules, and horses of the trains and pilgrims manage to exist is a problem. It seems to me that thousands must perish. All life, and all living things, seem to be gone. Stillness, desolation, and the elements reign. It appears like Idumea and Petrea, with God's curse that it shall not be inhabited by man. The rains descend, but the parched earth puts forth no vine; the mornings come, but, silent as the evening, no raven flies the air; we behold the watercourses, but we hear not the murmurings of the fountains. The Sahara can only be more desolate in size—not in quality. It was a Sunday morning—the mules at the station had got loose, and wandered over the sand hills. While in search of them I came across an abrupt ditch five or six feet deep, and of the same width, which had been dug out by some recent torrent. Following its serpentine course, I found a large ox, which venturing too near had probably fallen in, and was now lying upon his side in such a cramped position that he could not help himself. Poor fellow—he had belonged to some emigrant train, and disappearing in this way could not be found, and would surely have died in a short time more. We brought grain and water from the station—excavated the side of the ditch at a convenient point—got a rope round his horns, drew him to the proper place, and finally succeeded in getting him out. How long he had lain there, and where his companions were, we could not tell; we had performed the Bible's teachings of pulling the ox from the pit upon the Sabbath day.

It seems to me we ascend as much as we descend from the eastern range here. Since we left Denver we have not been out of sight of snow, which lasts the season through, and now lies within six miles of Salt Lake City. Strange to say, we have not yet crossed any severe hills. The grading of a railroad, in my opinion, would require less engineering skill than it has on the Erie, Pennsylvania, or Baltimore and Ohio roads.

The North Platte, the Green, the Bear, the Weber rivers, and several others, are fine streams, crossed by rope ferries, when not fordable—which is generally the case—for which the modest price of seven dollars a team is charged. Crossing from the Valley of the Bitter Creek to Green River, we pass the finest geological formation and most sublime mountain scenery upon which the eye of man ever rested. The whole mountain range appears to be of secondary formation—the top stratum of red and the lower of white sandstone. It is still in course of decomposition, and the elementary changes, apparently recent, are most novel, startling, picturesque, and grand. White granulated sandstone, with inclined sides five hundred feet high, support towering promontories of red stone of equal or greater height—perpendicular as a plummet, smooth in some instances, corrugated in others, and level upon their tops—the seams of the lower stratum running horizontal, while those of the upper are vertical. Alive in the sunlight and dreamy in their shadows for a thousand feet above our heads, they awaken the mind to a conception of the vastness of nature, and carry us back to the time when seas were surging their fury and mountains were lashed into these romantic resting places. We can picture forts, towns, castles, parapets, battlements—the Ghebers cliffs where the Fire Worshippers hailed the rising sun, or Oman's turrets, where daring Haffed "sought the gory vulture's nest, but found the trembling Hinda's bower," or anything which history suggests or the imagination inspires—grand—wonderful—sublime.

I was quite sure I should find photographic views of such wonderful beauties, but am again disappointed. Some artists went from here last season to Echo Cañon, and will this year proceed to this place.

On the very highest passes of the Rocky Mountains, say nine thousand feet high, I collected beautiful and compact marine fossils—salt-water shells, great solid hills almost wholly composed of the evidences of former sea life! At another station nearly as high, I took specimens of bituminous coal from veins six and eight feet thick.

At Fort Bridger, one hundred and eighty miles north-east of Salt Lake City, we commence to see vegetation, and in the foot hills composing the valley between the Utah and Wind River Mountains, are some fine grazing lands. About a half dozen varieties of the genus larkspur here abound; some of them are very beautiful. They are of all shades and colors, but yellow always predominating—more compact than the larkspur and more brilliant and delicate than the delphinum formoscum. These and the mountain cactus, before referred to, are the only flowers yet noticed that I would recommend to naturalize.

At Bear River we meet the first Mormons. They increase from here on. The farmers universally live in little one-story log or adobe houses, covered with poles and earth. I must say, they are much superior as a class to the habitations of the pioneers of Kansas, Iowa, and Missouri.

The celebrated Echo Cañon, say sixty miles east of this, where the Mormons once fortified to resist the United States forces, has high, precipitous, and sometimes overhanging red sandstone rock, on one side ranging from two hundred to six hundred feet; on the other, receding hills. It is not extraordinary. At its foot we strike the Weber river and the Mormon village of Chalk Rock. Beautiful small farms, all irrigated. Wheat and garden vegetables, no more forward this 7th of July than in Jersey on 10th of May; the chances of great success I do not look upon as bright. We rode in a heavy frost and severe cold the preceding night. Now comes thirty miles of the worst and most dangerous gully road, and the highest overlapping hills we have yet encountered. It was in the night. There was hardly room for the coach to pass the glazed rock on one side and keep the wheel on the narrow path beneath. Several times we had to get out to assist the coach. Had we made a misstep and tipped over, we should have landed among the jagged rocks and in a rolling torrent below—probably not in a condition to have penned this letter.

Just as the sun kissed the southern hills we emerged from the mountains, and looked down upon a beautiful extended plain, fifteen by thirty miles, and upon one border, some seven miles distant, stood the sleeping city of the prophet. Houses half hid amid dark green foliage, with curling smoke arising therefrom—not a spire to remind us of an American city—made a picture, soft, mellow, peculiar, and beautiful. As we approach we find the trees principally peach and apple, with a burden of fruit I have never seen equalled. The houses are almost all of large size, brick or "*adobe*"—the natural color of which is a fine, bright blue slate—

usually one story, but varying to two as with us. They all have high, prominent chimneys, and on large houses there are several. Some are plastered and painted—an additional beauty. The blocks are six hundred and fifty feet square, or over three times those from Fourteenth to Fifteenth streets, in New York. The streets are two hundred feet wide, crossing each other at right angles, with a running stream of irrigating water either on one side or both sides. The houses do not stand close together. The city might probably measure two miles in diameter; and while they claim 15,000 inhabitants, I cannot give them over 10,000—although of this it is not safe for me, a Gentile, to judge, for I am satisfied children and water are the principal crops of Mormon production. There are *a few* as fine stores as anywhere in the country, an immense theatre and court-house, two banks, three papers—two Mormon, one Gentile; a tabernacle church that will seat 2,500 (a new one building that will seat 10,000), and several—they say twenty—good public school-houses, the support of which, as with us, is effected by a general tax—rather a sorry consolation for rich bachelors.

Just think of it, ye celibate Josephs—shelling out your greenbacks to educate some poor scoundrel's children. And supposing the name of those children's mother was Calanthia, who, years gone by, jilted you in favor of the dancing clerk with the curling mustache, whom you always so abominably abhorred! Bah! what an ugly world.

Next to Jerusalem, Salt Lake City, away off in the centre of a vast continent, had seemed to me the most enchanting city in the world. I exceedingly regret that my Indian delays have cut my time so short as to limit my information respecting population, productions, civil codes, religious habits, social customs, etc. To come so far, stand so many jolts and scares, and stay but a day, is quite unsatisfactory. But I must leave San Francisco, by steamer, 1st of August, and I have much to do.

To the casual observer these people appear harmonious, polite, affable, and prosperous to a great degree. Their poor are cared for in a most praiseworthy manner. Liquor is not allowed to be sold in the city. The proportion of criminal convictions is small. Their system of government is not, as I had supposed, a hierarchy, but republican. Brigham Young, the President of the Church, is purely an ecclesiastical ruler, and has no authority whatever in civil affairs. First marriages, as with us, are optional with the parties, and may be performed by any officiating priest. Second and further marriages, anywhere in the territory, can only be performed by the President himself, and after such personal knowledge or statements from the local priests as justifies the belief of good moral character and ability to support the duplicate wife and children, *and with the sanction of all previous wives*, either by their voluntary written consent, or, when admissible, by personal attendance and affirmative answer at the time of the ceremony. The power of divorce also lies with the church. The men claim great sanctity of purpose and much personal inconvenience and expense in supporting several families instead of one. Where they multiply too fast, and the means will admit, each wife has her own establishment; but more frequently they all live together. They say the natural effect is to produce a larger number of children—an average of eight to a married female of thirty—a considerable preponderance being females. Nothing in the apparent physical or intellectual development of the youth or children indicates immaturity or decay. As to the principles of Mormonism, they are made for men. The women are timid and recluse, do not support many elegancies, or appear as the equals of men. You cannot catch the eye of the few females seen in the streets; and, singularly enough, I have not seen one who could lay the least claim to beauty. They are coarse and menial. In calling upon an old acquaintance of my boyhood, who had long ago embraced their faith, and whose house and condition are good, he did not introduce me to either of the three women in the room, all of whom I took to be his wives. I noticed he was called father by four hearty children between the ages of three and six, while several smaller ones were kicking about, and how many more were in the cribs or out of doors I durst not venture to guess. I knew the delicate, high-spirited lady of his first love, whom he deserted for this harem life, and could but mark the contrast in the development of those emotional sentiments which, say what we may, constitute the only real happiness of life. If Miss Margarette B———e, of Medina, N. Y., ever sees these lines, she will learn the present position of J—— S——.

Notwithstanding the evident physical and moral prosperity of this community up to this time, I cannot believe but that a general system of polygamy would retard civilization and work the downfall of any advanced nation. What can there be in such a divided relation to stimulate the pride, gratify the hope, or reward the affection, of a woman? Love, the great stimulant to all that is good, beautiful, and holy, in the human breast, gratified by proper attention for a brief period, then fanned by jealousy, crushed by desertion, and finally insulted by beholding the attentions to which its rightful possessor was entitled lavished upon another; and not only must the skies become darkened and the world a blank, but life loses its aim—the mind becomes morbid—material ends are neglected—children are not cared for—maternal love is not developed—death is a relief, and society is cursed in a rising generation without hearts. The present weakness of the Mormons is their strength. Brigham Young is very capable, and, although without any legislative authority, has sufficient moral power to control all legislation, and is, in fact, an autocrat. While he or his successors have the wisdom to be temperate, charitable, and devoted, with the power to control and make themselves appear in the light of martyrs for conscience' sake, I can realize how their followers may, in the main, be zealously honest—how men may preserve their ambition, and how women may sing praises with broken hearts. So long as inferiority of numbers, and financial and political weakness, exist among the Mormons, creating natural circumspection among their rulers, and a toleration toward others, and the elements of schismatic strength are not great enough to induce internal dissensions; I do not see why they may not flourish and prosper. But give them strength, power, and the contact of natural society, and they must decay with great rapidity.

President Young has from forty to fifty wives— exactly how many I could not ascertain. Some of them, old and widowed, he married for force of example—merely to give them the right of his support; and I am told, some of them he has never seen since the marriage or sealing ceremony. His premises, consisting of ten acres, are surrounded by a twelve-feet wall, and, besides his principal house—in which reside about six of his young wives—contain the tithing house of the territory, a chapel, and his private school-house, in which are now some seventy of his own children. He is a hale, hearty man of sixty-four years; perfectly temperate in all things—uses neither spirits, tobacco, tea, nor coffee; exemplary, democratic, and liberal. Being uneducated, his sermons are bigoted, zealous, direct, and tautological. He owns a vast property in real estate, interests in stores, manufactories, Eastern stocks, etc. He is the owner of the Salt Lake Hotel, the house where this is being penned. A lady informed me that she once saw him order forty velvet bonnets, all alike—an evidence of his impartiality, no doubt—but what a luxury, at thirty dollars apiece, it would be to a poor man!

The great temple, which is to seat ten thousand persons, and advance pictures of which have been sent throughout the world, is now only built to the basement story. A canal, twelve miles long, is being constructed to transport the granite of which it is to be built, and which is the only granite I have seen through all the Rocky Mountain range.

I had not time to visit Salt Lake, and bathe in its dense waters. It is eight miles distant from the city. It is four thousand seven hundred feet above the ocean, receives the waters of several large streams flowing from all directions, and has no outlet. Its water is the most saline in the world, and contains one-third pure salt.

MINERALS.

There are said to be fine silver discoveries near here. Representative Ashley, Chairman of Territories in Congress, arrived a few days before me, and urges me to visit Rush Valley and the diggings with him. I obtained specimens for future use, and am compelled to forego a more thorough examination. From the scarcity of wood, I doubt if mining can be made profitable here, although that will not prevent the trial. The Mormons endeavor to suppress any knowledge of the existence of minerals; but the soldiers and the Yankees have been here; the facts are known, the Gentiles are coming, and the Mormons will either have to migrate again or abandon polygamy and adapt themselves to the usages of American civilization. President Young is absent, as I understand, on a tour of discovery for a new Mecca.

A one day's sojourn is quite inadequate to collect sufficient data upon which to speculate, but the main physical features are as here presented, and the progress made is greater than I have observed elsewhere in my travels, with double the time and advantages in favor of other people and localities. But the high, pure mission of lovely woman, the incentive to man's ambition and his happiness, is gone, and the prosperity of man founded upon the degradation of woman I hope cannot exist—although the ways of Providence are marvellous to man.

VIII.

MORE ABOUT SALT LAKE CITY—LEAVING THE CITY—RIVER JORDAN—RUINS OF CAMP FLOYD—APPEARANCE OF THE COUNTRY—INDIAN LOVERS—DIGGER INDIANS—A MOUNTAIN MAID.

AUSTIN, NEVADA, *July* 14, 1865.

MY last was left in private hands at Salt Lake City, to be worked through overland, if possible.

The estimate of the Mormon population in the entire valley at 100,000 is about correct. The advantage which the settlement of that half-way house in the deserts of America has been to the people of the United States, is incalculable. Prices of everything consumable advance with terrific rapidity as you leave either coast, until met by the productions of Salt Lake Valley, where we find flour, oats, barley, potatoes, fowls, beeves, salt, garden vegetables, etc., in abundance, and at reasonable prices. The salvation of Mormonism, as an institution, depends upon its isolation, a fact which the apostles well understand. Under the circumstances, they treat the Gentiles with much toleration. The soldiers stationed near the city publish a daily paper—the *Vidette*—strongly anti-

Mormon, but which circulates by the side of their own papers, the *Telegraph* and the *News*. They discourage the development of the mineral wealth in their vicinity.

It is not for me to discuss theories, but simply to state facts. It would be unjust in me not to say that the progress of the Mormons in agriculture, manufacturing, and general development is immense, their physical comforts many, while ancient Nineveh alone, of all the cities of the world, could rival theirs in beauty.

Still further developments are to be made. Referring to the map, you will see that the Gulf of California and the Colorado river, receiving their first waters far to the north and east of this section, must ultimately invite transportation that way. Vessels will then lay their freight down from New York as cheaply at the head of the gulf as they now do at San Francisco. I understand steamboats can now be run within three hundred and fifty miles south of the city, which may still be lessened. It was a great mistake on the part of the United States in the Gadsden treaty, not to have secured the line across the head of this gulf. A large city is destined to flourish there, and its destiny must be American. Perhaps the change of a few degrees of boundary at that time might have saved us another Mexican or a French war. Young men, here is your place.

I am again seated in the stage at noon of my second day, and leave Salt Lake City with regret. Crossing the plains to the south on a perfectly straight road, I could, with my glass, look up the street I had left, and locate buildings in the city fifteen miles off.

We are all this distance upon a thickly populated road, with irrigated farms on either side. As before remarked, the houses are mostly one-story, *adobe*. We soon reach and follow the river Jordan for a few miles, crossing it at a width of one hundred feet and a depth of two to three feet. I quenched my thirst in its rapid and pure waters, and filled my canteen for future use. It runs from Utah Lake into Salt Lake, the latter of which has no outlet. At Camp Floyd, or Fort Johnson or Crittenden, as it is variously called, forty miles from the city, we turn westward, but not before recalling the memories of destroyed cities and deserted houses, which the power of armies or the devastation of earthquakes have pictured in our imagination. This place had been the principal Government depot and station for a vast extent of country during the Mormon war. From seventy-five to one hundred acres of land were covered with adobe houses, barracks, arsenals, corrals, etc. Streams had run through the wide streets, the stars and stripes had floated from the pole upon the main plaza—life, gayety, and music had charmed the sojourner, and added romance to the scene. Alas! how changed. All are gone. Roofs have fallen in, ends tumbled out, sides broken, windows without glass, the waters dried up, the pole flagless, the music hushed—not a man, beast, or dog to greet you; all as still and silent as the tomb. Thebes in its sand, and the Pyramids in their solitude, could not be more desolate. The broken walls looming against the evening sky awakened musings long to be remembered, and only broken by the crack of the driver's whip and the rattling wheels of the coach, as they rolled us on our course.

The physical characteristics of the next five hundred miles, from Salt Lake to the Sierra Nevada Mountains in California, will be best understood by comparing the country to a vast sea, interspersed with ridges of towering islands. About fifteen miles of undulating plain, then comes a chain of hills—five to ten miles across, and twenty to one hundred miles long—running north and south, and but few of them presenting any life or vegetation. Some we cross through not difficult passes, or cañons; from others we diverge in course of time and pass around. Sufficient of them are snow-capped to allow me to say, that since we approached the Rocky Mountains, on the eastern side, we have not yet been out of sight of snow. I say this country is a vast plain, although about one-tenth of its surface is rugged mountain; for, between the ranges looking up and down, the horizon is unbroken, and the mind cannot overcome a feeling that just beyond that particular hill, to the east or west, all is level again. The plains are mostly desert. They afford very little grazing. For thirty to fifty miles, emigrants, stages, etc., have to carry all the water they require, and for several hundred miles provisions have at all times to be drawn from each end. Forage there is none.

The course of true love is said never to run smooth. A pretty young squaw attracted my attention at one of the stations. By her side was Willow-Spring Bill. Both were silent. At the next station, fifteen miles further on, we saw Egan Howard, lying dead and stiff, his head well smashed to pieces. It appears that Howard wanted the squaw, and not succeeding in her worthy father's favor, he watched his opportunity and killed the old man; whereupon Willow-Spring, being a friend of the father, and probably not an enemy of the daughter, had this morning retaliated. No one cared. The Indian lookers-on enjoyed the fun, and did not offer to bury Howard.

Speaking of Indians—of all the filthy, stolid, degraded wretches I ever saw or heard of, these different tribes of the Diggers are the worst. They live on mice, grasshoppers, lizards, snakes, seeds, roots, and what they can beg of the white travellers. They infest every station. They sleep flat on the ground without even a stone or a brush covering. They cultivate nothing. Their clothing, beyond beads and moccasins, is literally nothing except what the few whites throw away. They present the most grotesque appearance imaginable. There were half a hundred collected at Kingston yesterday. Their hair is excessively thick, low on the forehead, long, coarse, bushy, and black—so much is nature's dress. Add to this simply an old vest to one, a single shoe to another, a part of an old coat or the waist of a dress to a third, one-half of a pair of drawers to another, a part of a blanket, an old shawl, or a coffee-sack upon others; while one big fellow had nothing under heaven on his person but a tow string around his waist, and some not even that; while others, whose luck in gambling had turned that way, sported two old coats and no pants—and you have a fair and true description of these miserable creatures, whom pea-headed missionaries are trying to teach the Bible. Bah! nonsense! They are not human. Among all the aborigines who have inhabited this continent since its discovery by Columbus, no one has shown sufficient genius to stamp himself upon the progress of the world. They have disappeared before the vices of civilization as fast as they have traversed from the East across the Western wilderness, like dew before the morning sun. They see the whites build huts and plant potatoes; they sleep upon the frozen ground and eat reptiles. They learn nothing, do nothing, but starve and freeze. Plenty of work is offered them in the mines, but they will not work. The Howard and Willow-Spring Bill, above referred to, belonged to different tribes. The method of gambling, which I here saw, was to pitch gravel stones into holes; the stakes—each other's clothes; and I candidly aver that I saw one wearing three vests and a full suit, while the fellow with whom he was playing was reduced to one leg of an old drawer!

Just as we enter Nevada we cross the Egan Hills by a cañon of the same name. Some valuable silver mines are now just opening, and quite an excitement prevails. I secured some specimens, heard the statements, and reserved my opinion until better able to express it fully and comprehensively. Here is the first approach to what may be called trees, since we left the east side of the Rocky Mountains. A kind of scrub cedar grows up in the gorges that will average about as much wood as a New York orchard of twenty years' growth— not more. Wood is the great want of this country. Around Austin they say it is plenty a little way back. I know better. I have been "back," across, and all round. It does not exist.

Here, too, at Egan, I got a splendid breakfast— waited upon by a perfect beauty of a black-eyed girl. Her house was tidy, mountain-flower bouquets upon the table, standard authors upon the rude shelves, carpets upon the earth floor, and she, refined, light, and bright as a bird. Of all the superb scenes of nature which I have witnessed since my departure, none can compare to a pretty woman in such a place as this. She deserves a better position, and, if I mistake not, the gallant driver who carried us away from the place will give one to her. Should this just tribute to the winning graces of this mountain gazelle, whose charms captivate even with a plate of johnny-cake in her hand, meet her eye, I wonder what the little beauty will say.

Austin (Reese River District), the great silver section of the country, requires study, comparison, and investigation, which I shall transmit in my next. This goes by San Francisco and steamer.

IX.

STAGE COMPANIONS—MINING—MILLS, WOOD, AND WATER AT AUSTIN—REESE RIVER.

VIRGINIA CITY, NEVADA, *July* 16.

I SUPPOSE there is little doubt in the minds of my readers by this time that I am the friend of the ladies. I own the soft impeachment, and am willing to make myself very uncomfortable at all times for their benefit; but, at the expense of my gallantry, I must say there are places where crinoline is out of order and babies become a downright nuisance! I supposed I was to be the only passenger from Salt Lake on; but upon starting, I found myself *vis-à-vis* with a grass widow and four children under eight years of age—as my companions. Each had a specific want at least once in twenty minutes, which divided by four, gave me a gentle hint exactly every five minutes. A stage coach, down gullies, over stones, up hills, and across ravines, is not the most favorable place imaginable for sound sleep. The first night—each one clambering for the soft place and crying over the accidental thumps, assisted by the gentle raps and kicks of the mother, who insisted upon their keeping perfectly still, and occasionally asking the gentleman if he would not reach the canteen or open the basket—was charming to a man who had six full days of sleep owing to him.

The next day the children were covered with molasses and the stage with crumbs; and if you have never been here, I will inform you that dust, deep and thick, is the staple production of this country. Our condition is more easily imagined than described. When night came again I wrenched off the middle seat, piled in mail bags, blankets, and shawls, and spooned them in. They were so well tired out, I heard nothing of them until morning. But the woman—dear me!—not gifted with Eve's gentle confidence, posted herself upright in the further corner, and insisted she would not sleep a wink all night; and I think she would have declared she had kept her word had I not had to climb out for her lost bonnet once or twice. The Lord forgive her awful suspicions!

I do not propose to speak fully of minerals, mining, and the comparative value of the different sections I visit, until I have visited all. I find preconceived opinions upon the subject liable to great modification; and I fear that I am rapidly getting in opposition to most of my friends at home as well as here, as to the ultimate profit of working mines.

As I remarked in regard to Colorado, there is no question in regard to the existence of large quantities of silver ore at this point, or of the fabulous amount which is sometimes taken from a ton of ore. The blind man and the speculator are satisfied with this show, but it is right here that intelligent inquiry commences—the width of the vein—its uniformity—its location—the kind of ore—the necessary manner of treating it—the expense of wood—amount of water—cost of forage, living, etc., must be arrived at, the most of which cannot be done in advance, and the only thing certain is, that you can spend a big pile of money whether you get much back or not; and further than this—in a country so awfully barren and unproductive as this—where not a kernel of a corn or a spire of grass is raised—one cannot stand still. The cost of mere existence is an immense outlay, and compels a person to move. The silver ores of this section produce less per ton than the ores of Austin; wood is eighteen dollars per cord here, and there it is ten dollars; yet these ores being free from galena, pyrites, sulphurets, etc., can be worked at much greater profit than there. Where there is no water power, and wood at these prices has to be burnt for steam and for roasting the ores, it costs something. The lodes near Austin vary from six to twenty inches wide at a depth of one hundred and fifty feet. Here the Comstock lode is seventy-five feet wide. The books show that over fourteen thousand lodes have been located in the vicinity of Virginia City—while there is just one that is now being worked. All the mines are on the Comstock lode. Inexperienced men cannot tell the difference. Lodes which look as well, and produce *specimens* which *assay* finely, are held at high figures, and have broken many owners. Fifty thousand dollars asked for a lode which really can be bought for a breakfast, is a wide discrepancy, but I think there are many such.

Mill-masters at Austin will tell you they can crush 1,500 lbs. of ore in twenty-four hours per stamp; that the product will run $100 to $150 per ton, and that the expenses all told, mining, hauling, and crushing, will not be over $50 to $60 per ton. A ten stamp mill, like most of those here, will cost say $20 to $40. This looks like immense profits; but there is a hitch somewhere, for in all this district there are but five mills—forty-five stamps—in operation, while the Eagle, Pioneer, Union, the Clifton, and others are not running. Those in operation are the Oregon with 10 stamps; Ware, 5; California, 10; Rhode Island or Hildreth, 5; Midas, 15; and this is all there is of the boasted Reese River, Austin, Amidor, or Bunker Hill mining region, where 7,300 lodes have actually found purchasers. My fortune in mines commences to dwindle. It is singular that I find no one else who is not hopeful—yes, sanguine. These five mills have in two years consumed all the wood for twenty miles. What would 1,000 stamps do, providing the experiment could be tried for a year? Wood would have to be brought from the Sierras 200 miles distant, and would cost $50 per cord. Water is quite as scarce, and all there is in Austin would pass through a napkin ring.

Two valleys. fifteen miles wide, running north and south, the Reese River Valley on the west and the Big Smoky Valley on the east, enclose the Touyeba mountains, say eight miles across ; some of the peaks have perpetual snow. On the west slope, in a cañon six miles up, is located Austin, with a dashing population of near five thousand. Here were first discovered the silver lodes, and from Reese River, as it is called, ten miles away in the valley—a little stream of only about twenty-four inches of water, which all disappears some distance below—it is known as the Reese River District. But upon the eastern slope of the range there have been subsequent discoveries made of veins outcropping from four to twenty feet wide and equally rich with Austin. Here are located the Astor, Starr King, Bunker Hill, Barnes, Sloan, Central Park, Bowling Green, Broadway, Union Square, Brooklyn, and other valuable lodes, and with considerable water-power. At Kingston, thirty-five miles distant, the Sterling Company, of which Marcellus Massey, Esq., of Brooklyn, is President, is now erecting a stone mill with twenty stamps and capacity of forty, the only water mill in the district, and the best of any description in the territory, unless it may be the Gould and Curry at Virginia. I examined the surroundings of this country with great particularity, as my shoeless horse will testify; and if Kingston, Bassfords Cañon, the Needles, Geneva, etc., do not soon acquire a name and reputation, then no lodes can in Nevada. I am so largely indebted to W. S. Duncan, Esq., of Austin, and M. J. Noyes, Esq., of Kingston, for courtesies during my sojourn, that I cannot refrain from tendering my thanks. I hope that my fellow-travellers may share a like hospitable reception.

You see I am leaving this place unfinished as I intend. My pen will undoubtedly return here.

One might better travel in Europe for news. I am near six weeks out. My latest from New York is June 15th. As I am now about twenty-four hours from San Francisco, luxuriating on pears, grapes, apricots, peaches, melons, etc., I feel it is more like home. Set it down as certain I have eaten one good meal. This jolting in stages, climbing mountain passes, descending into mines, collecting specimens, examining mills, comparing ores, collecting statistics, overhauling maps, talking with everybody, and then writing to numerous correspondents all night, does not make this a trip of leisure to me, but nevertheless quite in my line. I propose to sleep a week steadily after I get on board the steamer, and dream of my dear friends, far, far away, in their Eastern homes. May the time speed, is the wish of the subscriber.

X.

RELIABLE INFORMATION — WASHOE — NEVADA — VIRGINIA CITY—A NEW DRIVER—IN DIFFICULTY.

VIRGINIA CITY, *July* 17.

IT is very difficult to obtain reliable information in this section of the world. The population is largely made up of adventurers, and every man seems to have an interest in favor of or adverse to everything and every place. I have made it a point to ride at least one station with each driver who has carried us along. Passing through some rugged mountains, the driver remarked:

"Sound silver lodes in here."

"But I do not observe any water or wood for working the ore, however rich it may be."

"Oh! plenty wood back on the range; deliver here at $3 a cord."

"How far back?"

"Some ten or twelve miles."

"But I should think it would be worth more than this to haul it over mountain cañons, providing it cost nothing to preëmpt or cut?"

"We haul five cords to a load; that's nothing."

"I should think such loads would tip over on the hill-sides."

"We only pile it on three feet high."

"You must require very long reaches; how long are your wagons?"

"Fifty feet; d——d inquisitive," was his laconic reply.

He relapsed into silence, and not another word could I get out of him the balance of the trip.

So my source of information had dried up for the time being. I can give the very best of reference in the vicinity of Wall street, that this manner of stating things is not confined to the West. O dear, deluded, gullible New Yorkers! if I should whisper to you a hundredth part of the schemes—as baseless as Mrs. Caxton's brother's (Uncle Jack's) coal mines—upon which your financial hopes are anchored, how you would tremble in your shoes, and how anxious you would be to return to your yardsticks and your lapstones! But, as I have remarked before, I shall let you down easy, and only partially refer to the underground view of mining in reality. But when I see magnificent buildings, with two hundred horse-power engines, and scores of men pegging away for five years, seven hundred feet down on the ledge, and never a pound of "pay" rock, the temptation is irresistible to inform somebody that investments in the "Morning Star," "Anchor of Hope," etc., at two thousand dollars a foot, might as well be looked after. If I was in that business, how I would like to take a line of "shorts." It is much the safest way, however, if a man will gamble, to go straight to a faro bank. He will save much time, and will know a great deal better how the thing is done.

This is generally supposed to be the richest silver mining district in the world. It is known as Washoe, located in Nevada, on the eastern slope of the Sierra Nevadas, nearly six thousand feet above the sea. The famous Comstock lode is here. The "Gould and Curry," "Ophir," "Savage," "Mexican," "Chollar," and other celebrated mines, here have their existence. Virginia City alone has a population of some twelve thousand, and Gold Hill, two miles further on, three or four thousand more. Land is sold by the foot, apples by the pound, whiskey by the gallon, water by the spoonful, and dice, cards, tenpins, and billiard tables, are spread out by the acre. Something immense is Washoe. Exactly what is it? A great deal of prospecting has been done on the surrounding hills, many wildcat lodes located, but to this day "pay" ore has been taken only from one single lode. This extends for some three miles along the side of the mountain, and singly and alone comprises the entire mineral resources of a world-renowned region. The vein is very wide, averaging seventy-five feet.

The vein, mind you, is quartz, not necessarily all containing mineral; which, to the sad experience of many, it does not. The ore is found here and there in small places, but the whole mass has to be excavated and assorted outside. The expense is enormous. One claim has had good success for a time, while others, located each side, have found nothing. The case above cited (I omit the name) is a literal fact, and is the history of most of the enterprises that have been started. At a depth of five hundred feet I am led to suppose the entire ledge has run barren, and all the companies in operation have been prospecting at lower depths for a long while—near or about two years—evincing great courage, and mineralogists say, with undoubted chances of success, as no silver lode has ever yet been known to give entirely out. But I do not believe any rule exists as to mines, except the rule of uncertainty. No two have ever yet proved alike. The dip of the lode was at first toward the hill. It changed at an equal incline the other way—at some four hundred feet down—involving the necessity of new shafts, buildings, etc., and great expense. The tunnels, shafts, etc., are immense. I entered one tunnel twenty-five hundred feet—near half a mile. It required two years to dig it, and is not yet taking out ore. All the ore which is being reduced from these mines at present is that which had been left on the side drifts while sinking the main shafts.

The mills are not as large as I had supposed—one running eighty, a second seventy-two, a third sixty stamps, and all others from forty-four to forty-five stamps. They are located from one to eighteen miles from the mines, wherever they can obtain a little rill of water. The ore has to be hauled this distance in wagons. The Gould and Curry mill is located three miles from their mine. The quantity of water which these mills manage to get along with is surprisingly small. All the water of any mill here might be passed through a quart measure, while many of them, both here and at Austin, have not enough to fill the mouth of a jug. The loss of quicksilver for eight months by one of the mills has been exactly three thousand eight hundred and fifty pounds, and this the most perfect mill in the country. Gentlemen who have been talking about the over-supply of quicksilver may put their minds at ease on this point. Gulch-mining consumes over five times as much in proportion. Every courtesy and facility was afforded me by some of these companies for examining their mines, mills, and books, for which they again have my thanks.

Virginia City has many large brick buildings, is lighted by gas, and presents a busy appearance. Real estate is low and population declining. Two theatres, a concert saloon, one circus, scores of bowling alleys and gambling places, mostly represented by astounding bands of music, marked the attractions of the place on a Sunday evening. The climate is dry, cool, windy, and extremely dusty. From Austin here is thirty-six hours—the mountains increasing in breadth, the valleys remaining the same as all the way back to Salt Lake. No grass, trees, or vegetation of any kind are to be seen. All is sandy desert, or rocky, bleak, bald, and desolate mountain.

The thawed mountain snows that sometimes make streams running into the valleys are soon drank up by the thirsty sands, and neither man nor animal can ever here find the natural means of sustenance. Hay, feed, flour, meats, fruits, and vegetables have to be drawn from California. Wood averages eighteen dollars per cord at Virginia. To have admitted Nevada as a State, with an equal voice in the Senate of the United States with New York's four million people and diversified interests, was an unmitigated swindle never to be forgotten and always to be execrated.

DRIVING SIX HORSES.

The driver had occasion to stop at a wayside place, formerly a station, and I took the lines. The horses were fiery, lively fellows, the leaders real live mustangs. Presently they took it into their heads that it was time to go, and on they started. Before I could gather the reins, they were in a keen run down the hill; I pulling, yelling, and bobbing about on the high stage box like a rush in a wind storm. The harness of the wheel-horses had no breeching, and I did not think to place my foot on the brake, which is the only way to hold back in this country. So down they went, pell-mell, until I threw the leaders, and the other four horses, entangled in the harness, were all piled together, and the stage over them. I had succeeded in breaking the pole, harness, and almost everything breakable, and furthermore in convincing myself and fellow-passengers that driving six wild horses down a mountain side was not exactly in my line. The driver came up and swore lustily. I claimed I did pretty well in keeping the snorting Mazeppean steeds in the road, and not sending the entire load headlong down the fearful mountain gorge.

The probabilities are that some of my letters between Denver and Salt Lake have not reached you. The accounts of Indian barbarities back of me are frightful. No stage has followed ours since we came through the Rocky Mountains.

The delay in receiving news, either by letter or telegraph, is very perplexing to a person as anxious to hear from home as is the subscriber.

XI.

GOOD STAGING—THERMAL SPRINGS—GREEN FIELDS—BIG TREES—TALL MOUNTAINS—SNOW BANKS—MEN BURIED IN SNOW SEVENTY FEET DEEP—DONNER LAKE—SACRAMENTO—CALIFORNIA.

SAN FRANCISCO, *July* 25, 1865.

HERE at last! The Pacific fogs just a little to the west; the hills, sage-brush deserts, and Indians behind me to the east. If ever there was a happy man at seeing a yellow car awaiting him by the hill-side, that man was the subscriber when he alighted from the stage-coach, where the Pacific road connects, about thirty miles beyond Sacramento. The dust in California is a thick, dark red; and with no rains from March to November, its density under a July sun is something almost intolerable. We left Virginia City at 5 P. M.; nine passengers in the stage, four outside, all drawn by six fine horses. I must say this is the first real staging I have experienced. The roads, ascending and descending, cut into the mountain sides like an immense W, are smooth, hard, and so easily graded as to ascend without difficulty, and to go down, under full run, quite exciting to all, and decidedly under protest from the nervous spinster on the back seat. About twelve miles out we struck the Truckey Meadows and little water run of the same name. I think I am safe in saying this is the first patch of natural agricultural land we had seen since leaving Kansas. The sight of growing grass and harvested fields, under the antecedent circumstances, was most refreshing and cheerful. This river, like all others in this section, soon disappears in the ground. We are now in California. A little to the left we pass the Steamboat Springs. About two acres of ground are covered with jetting smoke arising from scores of different kinds of mineral springs. As we approach the valley from the hill above, it seems that here is prepared one of the caldrons in which the devil is to try his first experiments in human cookery. The puffing, gurgling noise is quite distinct, and the vapor forms a dense rising cloud. Were it not for the more famous Geysers in the northern part of the State, these springs would be considered curiosities of very decided wonder and interest.

The scene has changed. We are ascending the Sierra Nevadas, with forests upon their sides, population in their valleys, and eternal snows upon their summits. These, too, may be called the first trees approaching the dignity of forests we have seen anywhere in Nevada, Utah, Colorado, Nebraska, Kansas, Missouri, or Illinois, east to Indiana. As we get further on, and for the distance of say fifty miles, the trees assume a size, altitude, and straight, majestic appearance, unequalled anywhere, I believe, upon the surface of the earth. Their great, straight, towering, motionless trunks inspire awe and veneration, such as would be natural if viewing the ancient cedars of Lebanon, made sacred by the history of our Saviour and the footprints of the Apostles.

It was night, but the evening was pleasant, and an almost full moon was shining, giving shadow to the trees, distinctness to the scenery, and perspective to the landscape. These were mountains, actual Alps, piled one upon the other, with gradual, though sudden leaps—up, up, until the mind becomes dizzy contemplating their giddy heights. Almost upon the topmost level lays ensconced Donner Lake, cool and tempting, reflecting the rays of the moon in silver sheen. By its side are summer resorts, and on its placid bosom, as upon our own beautiful Mahopac, glides the gondola and yacht, eight thousand feet above the city of San Francisco! Trout in abundance tempt the angler's skill. This is on what is called the Northern or Dutch Plains route. Lake Tahopic, or Bigler, is on the southern pass, a few miles distant. Of course I did not see it. In these wild mountain passes there is something truly terrific. Giant trees are lodged—head first, top downward, and threaten momentarily to take another start; water does not ripple, but plunges, bound after bound, down the precipitous and rocky cañons, while immense rocks themselves have been displaced by the pressure above, and lay piled in dangerous shape and frowning ugliness. Our road, of course, seeks the lowest passes, leaving these immense peaks towering over our heads.

Snow, twelve feet deep, now impeded our progress. Think of it, O ye sweltering Saratogians!—remember this is the 17th of July. Our overcoats were extremely comfortable. But for some hearts what a history these snow banks have, for it was exactly here that, on the 14th day of January, two men, endeavoring to open the roads during a violent storm, encountered a snow avalanche from the peak above, and thus lost their lives. Their absence and object were known at the station near by. All the population for fifty miles spent days, weeks, and nearly months searching for their bodies. The snow was seventy feet deep. A tunnel had been cut, running within two feet of them. The wife of poor Reynolds went almost wild. Under the advice of friends she left her buried treasure, and sailed for New York by the steamer of May 1st. On the 14th the snow had so far disappeared, that both bodies were found standing upright close together, their arms outstretched, as if toward the advancing avalanche. Oh! excruciating moment!

Oh! torturing death! What must have been their reflections while thus imprisoned and before death relieved them? Reynolds' body was encased in a metallic coffin and immediately followed his wife. The other body was buried by his friends here.

Soon we were threading the Western descent of our road, here and there bordered by irrigating canals and little mining towns. The heavy pines of the hills decrease as we make a lower level, and are gradually supplanted by the spreading live oak. The valleys are little more than narrow cañons, the soil extremely sandy, and the agricultural products meagre. From the irregular course of the fencing we observe that land is here considered of little value, and is only reclaimed where irrigation is possible. Rain does not fall between March and November. The earth becomes a powder, ready to float in the air by the least disturbance, and passengers in the stage coaches are well calculated to define what dust is. Indeed, our coats, hats, dresses, hair, and skins were all one color, and the effect most disagreeable. We had reached the plains—only a few hundred feet above the ocean level. The thermometer stood at about ninety degrees. The dust has a dark-red appearance, adding to the otherwise unpleasant effect. I had never experienced anything like it, disagreeable as was the desert dust for the past fifteen hundred miles. But it was a foretaste of what all California is made of.

"O Susannah, don't you cry for me;
I am going to Sacramento, with my wash-pan on my knee!"

rang in my ear as the whistle blew, and I was informed "This is Sacramento!" From the stage to this point we had made about thirty miles on the Pacific Railroad—passing through a level, dry, parched, almost desert country, with here and there a live oak, but nothing like settlements, except little decaying stations where the railroad had previously temporarily terminated while in process of construction. I think I am now capable of saying that the Diamond Mountains in Nevada and the Sierra Nevadas in California are the only considerable obstacles to be met with in connecting St. Louis and San Francisco by an unbroken rail. This end is being pushed vigorously; five thousand laborers are now at work this side of the mountains, and it is generally accepted in San Francisco that they will reach Salt Lake City in three or four years, unless it may be a short gap on top of the Sierra Nevadas.

We approach the city of Sacramento through groves of peach, apple, nectarine, and figs, with numerous windmills raising water for irrigating purposes. Situated at the head of steamboat navigation, it has been a place of immense business, but the railroad has moved the frontier farther inland, and, like Albany, it must wait its day of regeneration. The streets are regularly laid out, well built, and evince evidences of enterprise and accumulated capital. The terrible freshet of 1862 has led to some extended dikes, which, until again tested, serves to keep property down and enterprise out. Providence, R. I., people have been here, for I dined at the "What Cheer" hotel, and the meal was just as miserable as you would get in Providence itself. I subsequently learned I had not stopped at the right place.

And now we were sailing down the Sacramento, in a first-class boat. I endeavored to be romantic, but I could not. Here, as elsewhere in this wonderful El Dorado, I was doomed to disappointment. Both banks are principally low and covered with a high species of rush, called *tulles*. Here and there a farm approaches the river, in which case the crops look only ordinarily fair, excepting fruit, which appears to thrive in unusual abundance. It is only five to eight miles back to the hills, which are wholly treeless and barren. I have since visited the valleys of the Petaluma, Russian River, Napa, Knights, San Jose (pronounced "San Ozay") etc. They are among the richest of the State, and fully represent the whole State in climate, productions, etc. They differ only in degree, not in character, from the Sacramento. Most valleys are narrow, from one to six miles. They are rich and productive when they can be watered. They are not divided by hills, but real mountains. These mountains, if not barren and verdureless, are mostly covered with stunted oaks, chaparral, chimisells or wild oats, and can only be cultivated where irrigation is practicable. The intelligent reader will thus easily observe that settlements must be confined to small strips of land, affording few inducements for the spread of social refinement and educational advantages.

This is harvest season. No green thing but trees meets the eye. All appear to be dead and cheerless. But the winter rains will again impart new life where any existed before, and I am well satisfied both the landscape and climate must be beautiful.

XII.

SAN FRANCISCO—FOGS—DOLORES MISSION—CHINESE—CHINESE THEATRE—SEALS—FINE HOTELS—SALMON—ALCATROS—SCHOOLS.

SAN FRANCISCO, *Aug.* 1, 1865.

THIS is, of course, the New York of the Pacific States. If New York glories in its Broadway, Central Park, Fifth avenue, and beautiful bay, so does San Francisco in its Montgomery street, unrivalled hotels, miserable fogs, cold ungracious winds, fine salmon, big seals, and luscious fruits. In all of these she is unequalled. It certainly is a marvellous place. Only seventeen years old, with a population of about one hundred thousand, and all the commercial and social evidences of accumulated wealth and refinement. It is very unfortunately located for ease, beauty, or comfort. It already extends over four immense hills, the soil is very sandy, the wind blows incessantly from about one P. M. until sundown, filling the air with clouds of dust. In those sections where the streets are not paved it is terrible to encounter. I have seen fences five feet high inundated by drifted sand like a northern snow-bank. For this reason, there is no white paint in San Francisco—not a square yard. Clothes cannot be dried in the open air in the after part of the day. The sand finds its way into houses, upon carpets and furniture, involving the temper of the housewife and the softness of your hair. Gardens have to be made artificially, and almost every evening, all night, and mornings until the sun gets well up, a dense fog drifts in, excluding objects from view, making walks and clothing damp—too cold to sit without fires, and hardly cold enough for them. This kind of weather extends to the rainy season, which is our winter. It is not then materially colder than in summer, and the rain principally falling at night leaves the days very pleasant. Roses, geraniums, oleanders, feuchias, arbutilans, cactus, etc., grow to immense size, and when watered are in full bloom twelve months in the year. A few miles north or south and fifteen miles inland up the bay, this wind, fog, and low temperature entirely disappear. To me it seems a great wonder that some other position was not selected for the site of the maritime city of the Pacific States. True, for some distance inland the hills dip immediately into the water, but making this distance, beautiful sites could have been obtained, and the most important consideration of all secured—that of throwing the city on the inland side of the bay. As it now is she has access to but one small neck of land lying between the ocean and parallel bay of San Jose, extending southward fifty miles, except by water.

The remnants of the Old Spanish Mission in the shape of long one-story adobe houses, with walls four feet thick, projecting piazzas, tile roofs, barred windows, etc., still exist in one of the back suburbs of the city. The church and all its surroundings are strongly characteristic of the day and habits of the promulgators of the ancient Catholic faith. It is an immensely long, narrow structure, without steeples, a crucifix upon top, heavy prison-like doors, three niches under the roof in the front gable end, in which are suspended one large and two smaller sized bells. The bells are hung, rafters held in place, doors swung, and all other mechanical support made by the use of pieces of raw hides. The paintings and chancel paraphernalia are gaudy. The statuary has been principally removed, and much that marks the historic renown of Mission Dolores is passing away forever.

Scattered throughout this Western coast are many Chinese, who find their homes, rendezvous, amusements, and base of supplies in San Francisco. Observed in the streets or in houses of Americans, they are always clean, respectful, and energetic. They have entirely appropriated one section of the city to themselves, and in the small houses, crowded alleys, and incommodious apartments, where the majority of them reside, you see evidences of great privation, hardship, and little elevation of character. They are, however, a progressive race, and make their presence felt. Many of their merchants are among the wealthiest and most respectable in the country. The women of all ages now here are generally openly depraved; yet in the lowest places, personal neatness and presentable attire are always seen. The Chinese men say they do not bring their wives with them. In all instances their religious custom compels them to ship the bodies of dead Chinamen to their native land for interment. Servants can only be secured from among them by an obligation to this effect on the part of the employer. Their theatre is a wonder, and characteristic in its way. Rough in its interior construction, it has ordinary seats raised circus fashion for about three hundred persons. They dispense with movable scenery, but a stationary scene crosses a raised stage at about twenty feet from its front, with two wide doors near the right and left-hand sides, covered by falling drapery, and between which and back of the actors is located the orchestra. The entire walls of the stage are decorated with Chinese hieroglyphics, between which and the label of a tea chest, my inexperienced eye could detect but little difference. The acting consisted of sundry individuals coming upon the stage through one door, and reciting some kind of an independent and most generally disconnected piece, some in irony, some comical, some serious, and then retiring by the opposite door. Meanwhile the orchestra, consisting of one string instrument, played with the fingers, and three kettle drums, kept up a most furious accompaniment, as little approaching music as anything could be and yet have any connection with the pantomimic representation before them. We first entered at nine o'clock, remained half an hour, then went out searching the town for wonders, and returned again after eleven ; remained another half hour, saw a continuation of the same play, and the same audience, pleased, attentive, and listening, who, we were informed, would stay until one o'clock in the morning ; and the piece, running through several centuries, is sometimes extended for days.

I can bear testimony to the Chinese being the best washers and ironers in the world. A lady with whom I dined, giving her orders to "Whang" excited some curiosity in my mind, which in all respects, when gratified, was entirely creditable to the Chinese race as neat, genteel, orderly, and willing servants. They wear clothes always ironed with seams in, and look as if they were just out of a bandbox themselves.

The next thing in order in San Francisco is to visit Seal Rock, and breakfast at the Cliff House. Eight miles back of the city, on the ocean, reached by a good road made over barren, sandy hills, is the promontory looking out upon the broad Pacific, here known as Cliff Rock, and a little further around to the North making the southern boundary of the Golden Gate. According to arrangements, my friend's carriage was at my hotel at seven o'clock, and with overcoats and wolf-skin robes, this July morning, amid a heavy fog, we made the Cliff House, chill and damp, at eight. Our breakfast in fish, meats, eggs, wines, vegetables, and fruits, was perfect and well relished. Meanwhile, O ye youthful wonder-hunters and museum explorers, what a sight was here to have gratified your curiosity and excited your wonder!

At our feet dashed the angry breakers of waters wafted, perhaps, from the very shores of Asia; while a few rods out in the ocean rose several large island rocks, as large, say, as the house in which you live; an immense number of big birds, gulls, pelicans, ducks, boobys, etc., hovering over them and resting upon the ledges; while fighting for their places, climbing up the irregular sides, sleeping in piles, singly and in pairs, quarrelling, biting, rolling off, and swinging about, were infinite quantities of real live seals, or sea lions. They are of all sizes, from the little one, such as you see at Barnum's, to the immense fellows as large as a horse, and weighing over two thousand pounds. They show very ugly teeth and bark like dogs.

The noise is incessant; the din uproarious. Certainly they are a great curiosity and very interesting.

No place in the States, New York not excepted, has four as large and well-kept hotels as San Francisco. Unlike the cramped lounging rooms in the Fifth avenue or St. Nicholas, we have plenty of room in every variety and style. As to tables they could not be better, and are waited upon by orderly servants of uniform size and orderly training. And then such salmon, cantelopes, and grapes! They are enough to make one's mouth water for months. Strawberries commence here in February, and do not disappear until November. Excepting peaches, the flavor of which is very negative, all fruits are equal to our own, while nectarines, plums, and melons are superior. Figs are rich and abundant. The prevailing grape at this early season is the white sweetwater, which in flavor is not far inferior to the Black Hamburg of our glasshouse culture. The purple grapes are not as good as our Isabellas.

A description of a visit to the wine-cellars would be without interest to my readers. They are on a large scale, and the demand is such for the wines, that nothing older than the vintages of 1864 is to be had in the city.

San Francisco has a method of numbering her streets which ought to be adopted by all large cities without delay. Commencing at No. 1, the odd numbers on one side and the even upon the other; they follow this rotation only through one block. The next block commencing at 100, the third at 200, and so on. If a person wishes to find, say 840, he knows it is but eight blocks from the commencement of the street; or if, then, at 500, but three blocks from his present position. Then again, in case of filling in numbers or dividing lots, it avoids half numbers or changing the numbers of the entire street. Now, Mr. Mayor, let us have your recommendation upon this point in our terribly mixed up city.

The beauties of our overtaxed community are also observed here in the shape of a State license tax for doing business, a separate stamp tax of two dollars per thousand on drafts and bills of exchange, a wharf tax of twenty-five cents per carriage when leaving a boat, etc. What a debt of gratitude the dear people owe patriotic politicians throughout the country! But the honor of a dime stolen from the public is so much greater than the dollar earned by honest industry, and the people themselves take such a placid satisfaction in wearing rings in their noses, that I mistrust it will be a long time before this will change. What do you expect would be the effect of elevating a man just once to executive office, too independent to owe supposed obligations to political parasites—too sensible to be cajoled, and too rich to be corrupted? Wouldn't the disappointed soreheads make Rome howl? How I should hate to be that man's wife! Certainly she would not know her husband through the thick clouds of calumny if he ever came up for re-election!

Alcatros is a high, round, barren, rocky island, containing three to five acres, surmounted by a strong fortification commanding in all directions, and is the Fort Lafayette of the harbor. Viewed from a steamer crossing the bay, and looking up against the dark chaparral sides of Mount Tamulpais, rising two thousand six hundred feet above the sea just across the Golden Gate—it makes one of the finest pictures in the world. If Staten Island was a Vesuvius how it would finish the landscape of our beautiful New York.

San Francisco, like the Roman Senators, does not forget her youth. She is justly celebrated for the number and variety of her schools for both sexes. The character of the public school-houses, in neatness of surroundings and architectural beauty and comfort, is superior to those of New York.

From Salt Lake, greenback currency is not seen, and gradually you again become accustomed to the jingle of real gold and silver. Nothing circulates less than a dime, and small items appear high, but in the matter of large purchases they are much less than I had supposed. First-class hotel board $3 per day, etc.

XIII.

CALIFORNIA—TILLABLE LAND—WOOD LANDS—CLIMATE—
PETALUMA—SANTA ROSA—HEALDSBURG—SONOMA QUICK-
SILVER MINE—THE GEYSERS—A HARD RIDE.

SAN FRANCISCO, *Aug.* 12, 1865.

CALIFORNIA contains one hundred and fifty-five thousand square miles, embracing thirty-three times the area of the State of Connecticut. I have seen its hills, valleys, woodlands, deserts, mineral regions, and its farming lands; have observed the character of its soil, the peculiarities of its temperature, and its various utile characteristics. As a whole, general sterility meets the eye, and the practical mind readily observes that its population cannot become dense. Involuntarily the question is asked, where and how do the immense herds of stock find pasturage and the means of subsistence? The inquiry was well answered last year, when it being unusally dry many thousand head of cattle and horses starved to death. The soil best adapted to agriculture does not produce better than in the Eastern States, while the insufficiency of title to land of any value, has much retarded development. The long intermission of rains makes crops very uncertain—sometimes plenty, at other times nothing—while the bleak, parched barren mountains lose their remnant of verdure during the hot season, until it really seems that cattle have nothing to feed upon but the decomposed earth. If I remember correctly, Mr. Greeley estimated one-third of the surface of the State to be tillable land. My impressions are that hardly one-twentieth will ever return the seed put on the ground. It is mountain almost everywhere; not mere ranges, like those of Nevada, but irregular piles, lessening here, increasing there, assuming all manner of uninviting shapes, and only interspersed in the main by narrow cañons or small valleys. The Sierra Nevadas, in the Eastern part of the State, from one base to the other by a direct line, I estimate at some forty miles. Commencing near the top and sloping each way, disappearing by the time the bottoms are reached, is good wood, regular Eastern forests, and these are nearly all that constitutes the wood land of California. In the north-eastern section of Sonoma county, bordering the coast, are what are known as the red wood (manzaneta) forests, and a few small patches exist elsewhere. It is hard for the Eastern traveller to conceive a new country without making it either heavy timbered or level prairie. Treeless, verdureless, barren sand mountains are hitherto unknown to him. This, then, is what makes the distinct difference in the landscape, gives the very diversified temperature, drinks up even the night dews, prevents summer rains, and must affect the results of financial investments. Some mountains are covered with thick chaparral, others with scattered scrub oaks, or cedars; others with patches of wild oats, while the majority are wholly barren and lifeless. As to climate—how singular that we never, or so seldom, hear anything correctly stated! Either the romantic license of the professional tourist, or the narrow prejudices of interested, inexperienced minds, color, shade, and over or under state effects, causes, and peculiarities, until it is hardly safe to venture an opinion upon hearsay. For one, I had supposed the general temperature of California was equable, mild, cool, and delightful. I left San Francisco at nine o'clock in the morning with an overcoat and decidedly cool. We travelled three hours by boat and dined at Petaluma with the thermometer one hundred and two degrees in the shade. Of all hot places on the surface of the earth, you can find the hottest here fifteen miles from the ocean. Although dated at San Francisco, I am writing this on the Mexican coast, immediately under an equatorial sun, and our thermometer, assisted by the refraction of the sunlight on the water, has not been so high by several degrees as we found it on the Russian river and the Geyser Mountain, one hundred to one hundred and five degrees in the shade during the long summer, and not even an evening dew, much less a tempering rain. I had several days of this kind of experience, and many degrees added by being exposed in or on a stage coach, or on horseback, over dry ridges, etc.

My health has hardly been sufficient for the task, and the great fatigue incident to my hurried trip has detracted much from my enthusiasm and enjoyment. But I hardly think my readers will allow their sympathies for this reason to stand as sufficient excuse for the lack of interest thrown into my letters. Be pleased to remember, dear friends, that I came unheralded; that my tour has been for business, not pleasure; that I promised you nothing to start with, and if you are disappointed as you follow me along, it will add to my regrets, but cannot create a consciousness that I have not faithfully recorded facts as I have found them.

Allow me just here to add what all my personal friends previously knew, that I have not the vanity to put myself before the public as a letter writer, in competition with those whose lives have been spent in acquiring the sleight of hand, as well as the information necessary to make their literary efforts either interesting to the public or creditable to themselves. Labor for myself, not writing for others, is my calling. If, in acquiring a little outside information for myself through this section of the world, where the financial current is now setting so strong, I have transmitted the least interest or pleasure to others, I am certainly recompensed for the extra labor which indicting these desultory letters has imposed upon me. Excuse so much that is personal, and now accompany me on

A TRIP TO THE GEYSERS.

The crab-like shape of the waters comprising the bay of San Francisco, form quite a little sea of themselves. First comes Goat's Island, Alcostra fortification, Pelican Island, covered with immense birds, many pleasant promontories and rolling sand-hills, and then we wind into the Petaluma river, about the size of the Raritan up to New Brunswick, and debark forty miles from the city, in the village of Petaluma, a place of two thousand inhabitants, and of great activity and business. We then stage for thirty odd miles, and both by boat and stage have been surrounded by a fine valley landscape of irrigated farms, wild pasture lands, and live oak openings. For miles together, these scattered branching oaks convey the impression of an old orchard of immense proportions. The crops are here considered good—wheat, I think, thirty bushels to the acre.

We have passed Santa Rosa, another beautiful town, laid out on the Mexican plan of a plaza or park in the centre; and Healdsburg, further up on the bend of the Russian river, and just before it turns westward to break the hills and find the ocean. I cannot repress surprise at the size, thrift, and apparent age of these valley villages. Our villages East occur at a distance of from five to ten miles from each other; here they are twenty to forty miles apart, and of course are centres for a larger section of country. Hence the difference. The Russian is a large, turbulent stream in winter, but in summer its running water is inconsiderable, and this frequently disappears, and after coursing its subterraneous passage for a mile or so, reappears clear and cool, and ripples onward in apparent delight. We first crossed its bed on dry stones, and then again two miles further up, in water a foot or two deep.

Leaving the Geyser road at Foss', formerly Ray's Station, we take saddle horses, and over hills of wild oats, scattered pines, and patches of chimeselle and chaparral, with St. Helena peak on our right and Geyser peak on the left, presenting a picturesque route, up, down, between, and again up hills until just on top of the last summit, and looking over into the valley of the Big Sulphur creek, we were started from our quiet by an explosion under our feet, and then realized we were at the Quicksilver Mines of Sonoma. Soon we were treading our way through the tunnels, down the shafts, and among the chambers of the only free native quicksilver mine in the world. In all other mines quicksilver is only found in streaks of cinnabar, *sulphurets of mercury*. Here it is equally interspersed with cinnabar and free metal, filling the cavities in the rocks. Opening a mine and getting lodes defined, roads built, buildings erected, and everything in successful operation, is not the work of a few weeks, but much longer than the uninitiated suppose. But about three men can work in one shaft at a time. At the foot of the hill at this place, down just eleven hundred feet, is the Big Sulphur creek, capable of furnishing all necessary power for mills, reduction works, etc.

In the valley, and contiguous to the mines, are six hundred and forty acres of the finest woodland I have ever seen, belonging to the company, consisting of immense pine, live oak, the beautiful yellow madroon, and the red manzaneta. Nowhere in California have I seen so much of utility and beauty combined. Venison and beef were swung in the trees—a universal market stall seen in this country only—where, singularly enough, flies are unknown and the climate does not taint. Our friend Scovill also breakfasted us on trout taken from the stream. The operations of this company have but recently commenced, and, compared with the "Almaden," which I afterward visited, the results of the enterprise must soon tell upon the commerce of the world. When we realize that ninety-five per cent. of all the quicksilver anywhere produced, comes from three sources—the Old Almaden in Spain, the Idrea in Austria, and the New Almaden of California—and that gold and silver cannot be amalgamated without its free use, as well as the many other indispensable purposes of science, medicine, and the arts, for which it is necessary, and the dignity and national importance of a new mine of this inviting character may be appreciated.

It is located but about six miles from the Geysers. I was compelled to spend several days in the vicinity, in the mean time following the top of the hill—a road through the cañon not having yet been cut—we proceed by a rough trail, on horseback, and intersect the road we had left at Foss', at the Hog's Back, a place long since recognized by tourists as one of the grandest in this wonderful country. A high elevation has been made, and immediately on the apex of a sharp hill—extensive valleys on either side—for four miles the road follows the serpentine, wild, and grandly picturesque summit. It is a ride long to be remembered. But now we again look over into the depths of the cañon beyond, thinking we could throw a stone into the creek, and wonder how a wagon is ever to reach the bottom. If you are on horseback you will wish yourself in a wagon; if in a wagon, you will wish yourself afoot; for you have yet exactly two miles to make, one thousand six hundred feet of descent to overcome, and thirty-five abrupt turns on the mountain side to prepare for. Foss drives four horses, with a stage-load of passengers, down in twelve minutes—has done it in ten; but we were near an hour doing it on horseback, half the time on our horses' necks at that. It is the most of a hill road I had seen this side of the White Mountains, and the first time I had fully realized just how high one thousand six hundred feet really was. But wasn't it hot! The sun scalding, the hot springs puffing and blowing, and not a whiff of air in circulation—and no iced lemonade or claret punch. I think, however, this is but the experience of pleasure-seekers the world over. I have understood Mrs. Nicodemus to say even Saratoga lacked some of the comforts of her own suburban home!

You have seen the wonderful Geysers described many times. Lieutenant Davidson did it officially, while Bayard Taylor, with his accumulated power of comparison, has correctly delineated them, and all persons of travel set them down among the "big things" of the whole world. Their utility is a little obscure; but I am inclined to think that, without a breathing hole somewhere for the interior heat, which, we are told, seethes and burns and makes iron, rocks, and all things molten lava at some forty miles depth, we should have more volcanoes than we have, and what place would come in for the first lava bath it would be impossible to guess. Let any man come here and witness bubbling caldrons throwing the masses of water two feet high, hot steam disappearing in the clouds, sulphurous vapors filling his lungs and nostrils, and the ground so hot as to warp the soles off his boots, and if he does not begin to have a salutary fear of death and the devil, he is different from most persons.

Imagine several little Gulches debouching into the large cañon within the space of a mile or so, and in each a great number and infinite variety of mineral springs, exhalations, and gaping seams, gurgling, roaring, puffing, oozing, rippling, steaming, and leaving all manner of incrustations, crystallizations, and composites; some of the water running as dark as weird witches' ink, others, immediately at their sides, of entirely different temperature, mineral character, and shades of color; and the sense of sight alone comprehends the wonderful, terrific Geysers. Then come their chemical distinctions, mineral characteristics, temperature, taste, medical uses, etc.; iron, sulphur, soda, acidulated alum, iodine, ammonia, epsom salts, magnesia, alkali, nitre, tartaric acid, with many other shades and combinations, varying in temperature from seventy to two hundred degrees, and capable of boiling an egg or cooking an Indian in less than a minute—all abound. Infallible cures for cutaneous diseases, rheumatic complaints, mercurial taints, and sore eyes, are abundantly vouched for. Indeed, one of my curiosities is a bottle of the famous Geyser Spring eye-water. I do not purpose to do anything like justice to this place, leave it with reluctance, and shall always return to it in imagination with pleasure. When the Pacific road is finished, it will be the summer trip for our New York friends, and second only to Niagara.

XIV.

Russian River—Spanish Titles—Soda Springs—Calistoga Springs—Napa Valley—San Jose Valley—Windmills—Almaden Quicksilver Mine.

San Francisco, *Aug.* 2, 1865.

HAVING procured a guide at the Geysers, we breakfasted at five o'clock, and at six were in our saddles clambering over the foot-hills, taking observations, and following the course of the Big Sulphur, or Pluton Creek, as it is more recently called, to its confluence with the Russian River. I am no mountaineer either by habit or inclination. Twice we were compelled to make the extreme height of land on one side of the creek; once on the other, with a numerous amount of zigzags, ups and downs, crossings, etc. Weary and hungry we were happy to rest our horses under a live oak on the top of the mountain, as we came in sight of the beautiful valley of the Russian river, and there drank in a delightful landscape. Nestling upon the further valley side lay the pretty little village of Cloverdale, shaded by its rich orchards of apple, peach, figs, and apricots, while like a silver thread rippling in the sunlight here and there the waters of the Russian river crept along in silence. Still further westward rose the blue contour of the Red Wood Mountains, while up and down the irregularities of the hills shutting in or enlarging the view of the valley, finished a picture of rare beauty. We watered our horses at the spring hard by, treated ourselves to some claret and limes, and descended to a farm house where we secured bread for ourselves and oats for our horses. Our host belonged to that class of men termed drunkards. The farm was conducted by the wife, a vigorous, smart, amiable lady, once handsome, and whose youthful days had been spent " as merry as a marriage bell " near the city of New York. Poor woman, how she cried while relating her trials and endeavoring to look hopefully into the future which overhung the fate of her little family. The farm was less than average in quality, poor in buildings and improvements, about sixty miles from water communication, and yet could be sold for $35 gold per acre. She was clinging to it as one of the things rum would not be likely to blast. When I advised her to sell it and pocket the money, and gave as my reasons that ever to be dreaded cloud hanging over the head of California pioneers, in the shape of an old Spanish land grant, which I knew was being silently worked out, and which some day might leave her homeless, her grief was really heart-rending. I could only point to the thunderbolt, but could not avert the storm. Men will not love their neighbors as they do themselves.

One false step on the part of the nation has carried ruin to many innocent hearts. The treaty of Guadalupe Hidalgo, after the close of the Mexican war, recognized the titles of hereditary claimants to grants of land made by the Spanish authorities, which had never been seen, known, occupied, or improved by the grantees. Surveys never had been made, boundaries and the quantities always uncertain. Subsequent settlements by the Americans made whole valleys valuable, when these supposed titles were exhumed, courts suborned, surveys made, and boundaries floated to where most valuable and the actual settlers ousted of their rights. In the latter respects the character of the courts has been changed, and land supposed to have been obtained for grazing purposes on some river bottom, cannot finally be located up in the mountains to gobble up some one's rich mines. Nevertheless, the evil to agricultural interterests still exists. Many are the miles of most beautiful valley land which is yet nothing but public pasture ground, from the inability to secure titles sufficient to justify cultivation. Actual improvements only ought to have been recognized by our Government.

Following the river down some twenty odd miles, we drank natural soda-water from springs on the bank, refreshed ourselves on peaches, grapes, and figs overhanging the gardens, and arrived again at Foss' at eight P. M. Fifty miles of horseback riding over naked hills, in a terrifically hot sun, is not a small task for an uninitiated New Yorker, and we ate our supper in weary silence. The next morning, at three o'clock, guided by the stars and the dim profile of Mount St. Helena, we were in a wagon bound across Knight's Valley, and secured our breakfast at a neat bandbox of a place known as Calistoga Springs. California is full of mineral springs and places of natural interest, consequently the objects of watering-place sojournment are too much divided to give striking preëminence to any. Calistoga, however, is quite delightful, and more has been done in a public manner to make it attractive than has yet been accomplished at our famous Saratoga. Numerous pretty white uniform cottages nestled among flowers, gravel walks, and splendid drives surround the principal hotel or eating-hall, while jutting quite into the grounds on one side is a sharp, pretty hill, surmounted by inviting cream saloons, and affording climbing exercise and an extensive view.

We are at the head of Napa Valley, well cultivated, fertile, and rich. Wheat is the principal crop, but grape and fruits form no inconsiderable part of the cultivation. The village of Napa, at the head of navigation, and celebrated for its natural spring of pure soda-water, is a smart, thriving place of some two thousand inhabitants. Taking the steamboat, we again turn toward San Francisco, some forty miles distant, pass the characteristic scenery already described as incident to the bay, stop at the Government Navy Yard, at Mares Island, and dine in the city at six P. M.

The next day we were again in the cars down the San Jose Valley at the south. After passing some ten miles of most uninteresting sand-hills, we strike a warm climate, beautifully cultivated farms, and many of the country-seats of the San Francisco population who can afford such a luxury. Hundreds of wind-mills are always in sight, whose business it is to draw water from numerous wells and force it through irrigating troughs to every part of the land. This is harnessing the wind to good account, and the traveller cannot fail to be interested in the sight, as much as the owners are in the results. They commence their labors regularly at about one P. M., increasing with great rapidity for three hours, when at sundown not a zephyr is stirring, and their outstretched arms stand powerless and still. Here is a fine chance for the Illinois farmers to learn a lesson, which I am surprised has not been done long ago. The little towns of Redwood, San Mateo, Santa Clare, San Jose, etc., are all pretty smart and active, while at the latter place we found a hotel equal in all respects to those of our Eastern cities. It is in these small localities that California has acquired the reputation of its agreeable climate. Here the thermometer does not vary over twenty degrees the year round, and with its variety of production, and ease of access, may well be considered a most delightful place for a home.

Remaining over night, we took a carriage early next morning for a visit to the Almaden Quicksilver mines—distance twelve miles. Quicksilver, unlike most other minerals, is not found in distinct veins, but in pockets or chambers of greater or less capacity. The smallest indications, spots of cinnabar like a pin-head, or veins no thicker than a knife-blade, are followed with great caution, without regard to inclination or direction, until the chamber is struck or the lode found false. Thus we found drifting from the main tunnel all kinds of lateral drifts—dug ways, deep holes, crab shaped chambers, connecting with other drifts, etc. The rock dislocated by the blasts is carefully removed to the light, broken into small pieces with sledge hammers, and everything bearing the faintest indication of cinnabar thrown into a pile for removal to the furnaces, some three miles distant down the hill. The expense of operating quicksilver mines is principally in obtaining the ore. The mineral-bearing pieces of rock are simply put in a large furnace, heat applied, and the vapor condensed by coming in contact with water coolers. This precipitates the quicksilver, which runs out into kettles, and is put in old-fashioned Spanish iron flasks, containing seventy-six and a half pounds each, an iron screw forming the stopper, and that is all. No chemicals, no amalgamators ; simply fire and water. A stream of quicksilver running from the furnace into the iron receivers, is a pretty sight.

These mines were opened in 1848, are worked by a joint stock company with a capital of eight million dollars—produced about two million dollars of returns last year, and are the most productive mines in the world. Will some one please inform me why this stock is selling at fifty per cent. on its par value ? I think I could tell were I disposed to. The public know literally nothing about distant corporations. As to this mine, over sixty different tunnels have been dug into the mountain—only two of them are working. It costs as much to dig false tunnels as true ones, to excavate barren rock as pay rock ; but the outsider is led to suppose that the cost of smelting the small pieces of ore which are put in the furnaces, is all there is of it. Eighty thousand dollars was expended on a single one of these tunnels which never produced a cent. Then the majority of the rock brought from tunnels which do pay is barren, broken to pieces, examined and thrown away. Instead of saying, so many flasks of quicksilver were produced from fifty tons of rock, it ought to include the entire excavation, which would be five thousand tons of rock, etc.

XV.

My Opinion about Mining—Recapitulation.

San Francisco, *Aug.* 2, 1865.

I LEFT New York June 7, have visited the mineral sections of Colorado, Utah, Egan, Reese river, Washoe, and portions of California ; have submitted to an involuntary detention of several days by the Indians, attended to my private business in different localities, and by clipping a little here and there, and turning night into day, shall be able to take the steamer to-morrow, August 3, according to my original programme.

And now, to sum up and recapitulate. When I was a boy, I shared the youthful delusion that a bag of gold always existed away off where the rainbow met the ground. There always exists a controlling element in the minds of men that fortunes are sure, and everything on an immense scale, away off somewhere. Furthermore, to really dig gold and silver first handed, without the struggles of intermediate and second-hand effort, is very attractive, and so we of the East have been rushing westward, allured by the fortunes of a few lucky ones, and the sanguine descriptions of Uncle Jack's astounding prospectus, until discrimination is lost sight of and common sense appears at a discount. That gold, silver, copper, lead, etc., exist throughout this western country in fabulous amounts, is beyond a question; and I have but little doubt that the entire desolate ranges of mountains, extending from British America on the north to Terra del Fuego in the south, contain more and richer deposits of precious metals than are to be found elsewhere upon the suface of the earth.

But my observation has taught me that population—a large crop of men and women, all of whom in our civilized country have numerous wants to be supplied and whims to be catered to, from a paper of pins to a plough or a waterfall—is the true material out of which money is most easily and most surely coined. A merchant is not apt to trust his business to the most brilliant graduate of a mere theoretic commercial college, but relies wholly upon the ability obtained by practice. The same rule ought and must apply to mining. The best of mines will be of indifferent success while in the hands of these would-be scientific adepts, but who really are in turn humbugs, spendthrifts, egotists, and dead weights. Young men must grow into these places by degrees, and the person who directs a mine should have commenced by handling a pick. I believe that is the way our stores are managed; while I am equally certain it is just the way most mining enterprises are not managed. Works should be commenced reasonably small, and expand only on the basis of success already obtained. The country where most mining is carried on is very desolate, agricultural productions mere nothing, and consequently everything required very expensive. Where no productive industries exist, and all men turn speculators, morals are soon undermined, and few resist the influences or remain capable of telling the truth or of keeping a contract. If it costs one hundred dollars to get ninety dollars out of a mine, the result is quite as disastrous as if the loss was made in selling shoes or dry goods. This need not be the case, but that it most frequently is, is indisputable—not from want of ore, but from bad management and rascality. Look at the position of the mining regions. From the Missouri river to the Rocky Mountains, six hundred miles, is a vast rolling plain so circumstanced as to atmospheric effects, soil, wood, and water, that the majority of the last three hundred miles cannot ever produce anything to live upon; one hundred and fifty miles through the mountains to the North Platte, the altitude renders the climate inhospitable and the summers too short to ripen crops. Thence two hundred and seventy-five miles to Bridger is a terrific barren desert. From this to Salt Lake, one hundred and eighty miles, is a high, broken, irregular grazing country. Snow fell to the depth of six inches on the 18th of June. From a little beyond Salt Lake to the Sierra Nevadas, five hundred and fifty miles, there is literally nothing but barren sterile hills and desert plains, in which a rabbit must be dexterous to obtain one meal a day. What little wood now exists will soon be exhausted, while the streams all sink in the soil soon after leaving the mountain cañons. Provisions and supplies have to be hauled in the different localities from one hundred to eight hundred miles.

The mineral lodes themselves are far from being uniform. They are always located in some out of the way place, and assume all kinds of fantastic shapes: some rich, acceptable, and quite regular in quality; others capricious, poor, lean, and wholly barren in spots. The ore itself is more capricious still, and, from the admixture of base metals, pyrites, sulphurites, galena, arsenic, etc., resists decomposition or refuses to amalgamate, thus defeating theories, increasing expenses, and destroying profits. Money, skill, and patience are required to reduce the business to that general basis or standard upon which the law of chances or insurance can be applied. It is largely to the interest of the country that these minerals should be developed, and those who have risked their own money in such enterprises are entitled to the nation's thanks. Unfortunately, however, there is a way of making these risks on other people's money, which, like all joint stock operations, leads to carelessness, inattention, extravagance, and robbery.

The amount of precious metals, compared with the wealth of the country, is at all times very small. In 1860 we had only $330,000,000 of gold and silver in the whole United States, while the cities of New York and Brooklyn alone were assessed $800,000,000. The permanent addition of $165,000,000 of metallic currency would double the current value of all the property in the country in a short space of time. Such was the impulse given to the commerce of the world after the discovery of gold in California and Australia, that its real prosperity, development, and accumulation of distributed wealth, may be dated from that time. Hence, I say, we are all interested in telling the exact truth in regard to these new mineral fields— in sending the right men there, with the right instructions and sufficient means to dig ore, overcome the natural obstacles, and, by making money for themselves, enhance the value of our own properties. Many have said to me: Why speak so plainly and discouragingly of mining enterprises? I had the utmost confidence in these mines, and have very large investments in them. I came here to find out things for certain, not on a guessing expedition. I do not believe in hunting for larks in January, shipping coals to Newcastle, or in sending fools to Nevada. Undue enthusiasm and impractical judgment has peopled many of those places with a class of men incapable to perform what they too immaturely commenced, and, by their failures, have not only ruined themselves and friends, but have damaged the reputation of the mining country irreparably.

If you have the right kind of a practical man (hard to find), and plenty of money to back him, select your lode, work it for a year in some other person's mill, define its quality, then go ahead. Unless you have the two first, and can afford to wait a reasonable time for results, let the whole thing alone.

I may be wrong, but it strikes me this is the kind of information our people want, and, I am sorry to say, seldom obtain.

To-morrow I take the steamer for New York. My stay in San Francisco has been short, but interesting and agreeable. Her citizens are liberal, public spirited, and progressive. I desired to visit Oregon, but am unable to do so. The lack of information from home concentrates my feelings there to such an extent as to make me hurry up the few hours which now intervene before my departure, and the last morning dawns before I touch my couch. A telegram or a letter would relieve me much, and might prolong my stay, although I had engaged passage on this steamer by telegraph from Salt Lake before I arrived.

XVI.

Leaving San Francisco — Privateer Shenandoah — Steamer Companions — Children — Whales — Lower California — Acapulco — Death at Sea — Steamer Fare.

At Sea, Off Mexico, *Aug.* 13, 1865.

Steamer day is a great event in San Francisco. "Going to the States," as they call it, is the longing desire of almost every inhabitant there. Those who cannot go have friends who can, and it seems as if the whole city came down to see us off. I found a half dozen cases of wine had been sent by kind friends to my room, and other luxuries were provided in profusion.

At last the hour arrived—the city was hid behind the hills—we passed the Golden Gate and were upon the blue Pacific. The privateer Shenandoah has just destroyed thirty whalers up in the Northern Ocean, the news of which reached San Francisco the day before we started. It was the belief of returned captains that the Shenandoah had tacked her course, and was then laying in wait for our steamer and treasure, down the coast. It created great consternation, and several passengers refused to go. The Government agent despatched

the Saginaw, the only war steamer in port, to escort us to Panama. She was very slow, and we had to lay by for her during the afternoon. At evening she was some distance astern, and the next morning was not to be seen. Our captain had made up his mind to take the chances, and gave her the slip. We took a long outside course, and was out of sight of land for several days. On the afternoon of the fifth day smoke was seen in the distance which soon grew into a steamer, and news came back to the cabin where I was writing that the Shenandoah was bearing down upon us. In an instant everything was excitement. Every glass was pointed and every kind of fear expressed and speculation entered into. Appearances were against us. My luck—Indians by land and pirates by sea. Trunks were hastily filled, valuables put out of sight, and babies got in order. We had two guns which were unlimbered and shotted—what for I could not divine, for we should only have added to our misfortunes by trying to fight a war vessel. One spinster lady of middle age—literary, I mistrust, from her peculiar ways—had put up her book and come on deck with bonnet, vail, and gloves, a bandbox in one hand, a valise in the other, waiting for the attack. She seemed anxious to surrender, and I was irresistibly reminded of the young lady who, when the town was besieged, asked her aunt—
"When will the ravishing commence?" The stran-

ger fired a gun to bring us to, and we came within close range before she was made out to be the United States steamer Wateree, which had hailed us for news. She boarded us in true man-of-war style, and when we parted she saluted us with a gun, and we her by raising and lowering our flag three times.

I am not in the least opposed to populating the country in a reasonable manner, if the rising generation can be kept in their proper spheres; in fact, I plainly realize that manufacturing dry goods would be a slim business after a while, if children were interfered with; but children on an ocean steamer, in a hot climate, are a most infernal nuisance. There were exactly thirteen babies belonging to rooms in my quarter of the cabin, and this appeared to be a specimen of the boat. First, they get sick and vomit, then they get the prickly heat and squall; finally they get whipped and yell. They wallow on the floor, they climb into your chair, they stop up the gangways, they are bound to fall overboard or down the stairs, and keep the mothers in a stew, and everybody else very uncomfortable. A woman with a child is just no company at all. You can't talk to her—she won't listen; she can't talk to you—it is "Susa don't do so," "Susa want a drink?" or, Jimmy this and Jimmy that—breaks in everywhere as if the whole world had a particular interest in this particular child, and were willing to sacrifice their whole time and pleasure to the thoughtless demands of a nervous mother, and for no good. With no disrespect to the ladies, I plainly suggest there is much which they can beneficially learn upon this subject.

Our company had now become somewhat acquainted. After one day, with occasional exceptions, the sea was smooth—the moon was bright; we happened to have musicians on board; the deck was frequently cleared and dancing made the evening merry as a marriage bell.

Many whales were seen during our voyage. I saw one large black fellow pass close to our starboard side, which exposed a perpendicular head of ten feet and a back of fifty feet out of water. One morning early the ocean seemed to be alive with black porpoises, or horse-fish, as they are called. They are five to ten feet long, very pretty in shape, and produce a half barrel of oil. They were all jumping out of the water in one direction, and, could they have been counted, I venture the opinion that one hundred thousand were in the air at one time, in an area of five miles.

We sail along the coast of Lower California. It is barren, mountainous, almost treeless for its whole extent. Early on the morning of the seventh day we entered the land-locked harbor of Acapulco, Mexico, in the face of Fort San Diego, which the French had battered to pieces a few months ago. There are no docks. We anchor in deep water and take in coal from lighters. There is no good coal on the Pacific coast, and that which the Steamship Company use is brought from Pennsylvania. A party is made up to go on shore in a small boat, and I had the pleasure of playing the agreeable to a lady of superior culture and intelligence. Passing the numerous native boys, who apparently live in the water and dive for coins thrown in at a depth of many feet, we salute Maximilian's representative on the beach, and then do up the town.

Acapulco forms one point of a triangle between Vera Cruz and the city of Mexico, being about four hundred miles west of the former, and two hundred miles south-west of the latter place. It has not to exceed two thousand inhabitants. The hills immediately back of the city soon rise into granite mountains of volcanic character which shake the place to pieces once in about ten years. It is located in the torrid zone, and is said to be the hottest and most unhealthy place in America. We tread upon our shadows to the south at noon. This place was founded one hundred years before the pilgrims landed upon Plymouth Rock, has the best harbor upon the Pacific coast, and is the principal western seaport of the empire of Mexico; and yet, when I endeavored to secure some kind of a conveyance to go into the back country, I found there was not a wheeled vehicle in Acapulco, or any wagon road leading out of it! All of the intercourse and transportation of the country has to be done upon pack mules over mountain trails, just as they were marked out by the buccaneers in 1520. I saw a train of some half dozen mules come in in this way, each with a three hundred pound bale of cotton upon their poor backs. What hope is there for such a people except in extermination! Improvident, intolerant, and extravagant, they all resist mechanical and utile innovations, and do nothing to improve the rising generation. I saw nothing growing except indigenous plants, among which are the bananas, cocoa-nut, oranges, limes, alligator pears, and maringos. The few shops contain nothing but imported goods, and the only articles I could find worth bringing away of domestic production, were cigars and strings of sea-shell beads, unless it might have been some black-eyed señoritas whom I saw in a house where we called for water. A mother and four daughters were present; hoops were dispensed with, and no superfluous dress encumbered or concealed the symmetry of their forms. All were beautiful, but one was angelic. They were cultivated and refined, but could not converse in English. They brought us water from a large earthen jug set in the ground; some cake and home-made taffa. Their pantomimic efforts to make our stay agreeable were entirely successful. Peace be unto that house.

We wandered in a cocoa-nut grove, visited the old fort, and dined at a miserable restaurant—the best in the place—upon chicken, eggs, bread, fruit, and coffee. When I asked for butter, milk, and ice, they laughed at my verdancy. I saw just one man at work—he with a cigar in his mouth—pretending to lay up the wall of a house. Maximilian's military forces were being reviewed under a piazza. They consisted of just fourteen men, no two of a size, and of irregular uniform. What a farce! The houses are built either of bamboo, and open sides to let the air through, or very thick stone or dirt wall to condense atmosphere. Lazy men and women were swinging in hammocks in the shade, while nude children were wallowing in the streets or bathing in the water.

At four o'clock a gun from the steamer warned us on board. We had to carry the ladies over wet planks across the beach into the skiff, and then pull and lift them up the side of the vessel upon the deck. Hard work for warm weather; but we did our duty like men?

Six days more and we are in Panama. We have been frequently in sight of islands and the main land—always hilly and no traces of cultivation.

A French military officer died at three o'clock.

His remains were sewed in a sack, with a weight tied upon the feet, placed upon a board, and at ten o'clock at night we committed them to the deep from the stern of the ship. One splash, and all was over. A hard, cruel proceeding. The engine ceased for less than a minute, but the motion of the vessel was not stopped, and the body fell flat upon the surface of the water, and floated off in the distance instead of sinking immediately out of sight.

We hear a great deal said about the splendid living upon these steamers. I desire to say that they are better than on the Atlantic side; but both are a disgrace to civilization. We were on the new steamer "Colorado," and under a favorite commander. The captain and purser insulted the entire company at every meal by having extra dishes, iced butter, milk, etc., for themselves and friends; while others, sitting at the same tables, had running butter, no milk, brown sugar, and limited supplies of other things. The chunk beef and bacon, given to the second-class passengers, were so foul that no human being could take them into his stomach. This was not accident but design—repeated day by day. I made it my business to find these things out. Oh! how the poor steerage passengers do have to suffer and humiliate themselves! I would like to see some avenging thunderbolt palsy the upstart sneaks who make weak women eat filthy meat standing; who compel them to sit upon the floor in a hot sun if they want pure air, and who heap upon them and other unfortunates indignities which make my blood boil to witness. It is very usual to bespatter commanders of vessels with fulsome praise, and the thing was proposed on this occasion in the shape of complimentary resolutions by some of the passengers, who thought a glass of wine with the captain at the last dinner a great honor ; but I squelched the thing squarely by saying, in his presence, that I should first require a letter from the captain to his passengers commending our forbearance in not openly resisting his insults. It was quite difficult for me to keep my hands off some of these fellows several times.

XVII.

PANAMA — THE ISTHMUS — ASPINWALL — CARIBBEAN SEA — ST. DOMINGO — CUBA — SANDY HOOK — HOME.

STEAMER OFF CAROLINA, *August* 20, 1865.

IN thirteen days from San Francisco we anchor under Perico Island, three miles from Panama, and go ashore in small boats. I obtain three hours to see the city, which is purely Spanish, with narrow streets, a cathedral, a college, several large but cheap churches, and others in ruins—all Catholic, of course ; no other buildings of note. Population not to exceed six thousand, although it has been more. The ancient town of Panama, which is several miles south of this, was destroyed by the buccaneers in 1670, and is now nothing but a heap of ruins.

On an open plaza near the sea wall is a large public well, where women come to wash clothes and carry away water in earthen pitchers. In true oriental, non-progressive style, there is no means of raising the water except what each comer extemporizes at the time. Piles of clothes, and a hundred turbaned women with baskets, tubs, or water-pitchers upon their heads, and countless little urchins rolling about in a state of nature, present a scene novel, if not interesting. In all these Spanish countries we notice many old-fashioned spotted lepers seated about the corners asking alms. One fellow here besought charity, who was smoking a good cigar, as if receiving gifts was wholly an honorable business. A few uninteresting photographic views were the only things of local interest which I could find to carry away. Panama is not what may be termed hot; the nights are cool. I do not believe it is unhealthy.

We crossed the isthmus in two hours and a half. Here, again, I was much disappointed. I supposed the forests were dense, and that we surmounted high lands. Upon the contrary, there is not a ten-feet cut or a tunnel on the road, and nothing in the make of the country that reminds one of an ascending or a descending grade. Hills appear in the distance, but the route taken by the road—which is only forty-seven and a half miles long, and, consequently, nearly straight—is as level as an undulating prairie. I could not ascertain what elevation is made, but it cannot be much; and I am confident a canal will some day pass European and Asiatic commerce through this gate of America. The Tuira river, further up upon the western coast, is navigable one hundred and two miles, while the Chagres, on the eastern side, is navigable for sixty miles. Trees, too, are scarce and small. The principal face of the country is covered by weeds, bushes, and small-sized scattering trees, the two species of most interest being the slender cocoa-nut and the spreading bread-tree, with their immense caskets of fruit. We stop at four or five little native villages. composed entirely of bamboo huts and thatched roofs. Not ten acres of land appear to be cultivated on the route. We followed the Chagres river, running to the east, for some distance before I knew which way the current ran, and I did not know when we arrived at the dividing ridge.

The temperate atmosphere of this tropical climate—its undulating surface, and its capacity of production—must make Central America a healthful and wealthy country, if it ever secures an enterprising population. The small State of Panama alone, which contains 29,000 square miles, and is only the size of South Carolina, has 149 streams flowing into the Atlantic, and 326 into the Pacific, and two considerable ranges of broken mountains. Indigo, coffee, tobacco, cocoa-nut, rice, maize, plaintains, valuable dye-woods, etc., grow spontaneously.

Aspinwall seems to be very low, and the other end of the same low land upon which Panama stands. It consists of a single street of cheap wood buildings, principally hotels and restaurants. Connected with, and extending down the bay, is the old Spanish town, formerly called Colon. Here is the Post-Office where I went to inquire for letters. I had to go around to a back door, get behind the desk, look the letters over, and help myself.

This is the rainy season. It sprinkles—sometimes rains for a few minutes; the sun then shines furious and sultry for half an hour, and then another cloud and rain.

We arrived at Panama anchorage at seven in the morning. We leave Aspinwall at five in the afternoon. And now, with an additional passenger list, we are crowded on the little steamer Costa Rica, which, so far as I can judge, was built to see how uncomfortable passengers could be made in a warm climate. The cabins are perfect enclosures all round —not an air opening anywhere. The living is horrid, and we are all incensed. The rain continues by spells for two days. We cross the Caribbean sea, make the island of St. Domingo to our right and Cuba to our left, and the eighth day from Aspinwall—the twenty-third from San Francisco— at two in the morning, we behold Nevesink light, lay off Sandy Hook until daybreak, take on a health officer at Staten Island, and reach the Canal-street dock, in New York, at eight o'clock. I drive to my office with speed—I meet old friends—I behold you, dear reader, turning the corner, and all things seem new, fresh, and full of joy and beauty to me. I left New York on the 7th June, have encompassed what I have written in these letters besides my private business, travelled over eight thousand miles, and am home again well and thankful this 25th day of August, 1865.

Demas Barnes.

www.ingramcontent.com/pod-product-compliance
Lightning Source LLC
Chambersburg PA
CBHW031324160426
43196CB00007B/657